ALPINE POINTS OF VIEW

ALPINE POINTS OF VIEW

a collection of images of the Alps

by

Kev Reynolds

ISBN 1 85284 460 4
A catalogue record for this book is available from the British Library.

Printed and bound by mccgraphics – Artes Graficas Elkar S. Coop.

DEDICATION

for Ernst Sondheimer, the most generous of friends

ACKNOWLEDGEMENTS

My thanks to all those friends with whom I've shared countless days of activity in the Alps in the past four decades, but especially to my wife, whose love and continued support makes each trip both possible and worthwhile. I am also grateful to Peter Wells and his staff at Contact Prints in Oxted, Surrey, for producing the prints for the layout of this book, and to all the team at Cicerone Press for turning it into reality.

Kev Reynolds

Cover photo: Evening light on the Mont Blanc range, seen from Cabane du Mont Fort
Frontispiece: Tiny Lac Flégère on the flank of the Aiguilles Rouges, with its view of the Grandes Jorasses, Rochefort arête and Dent du Gént, with the Grands Charmoz and Aiguille de Blaitière in the middle distance

CONTENTS

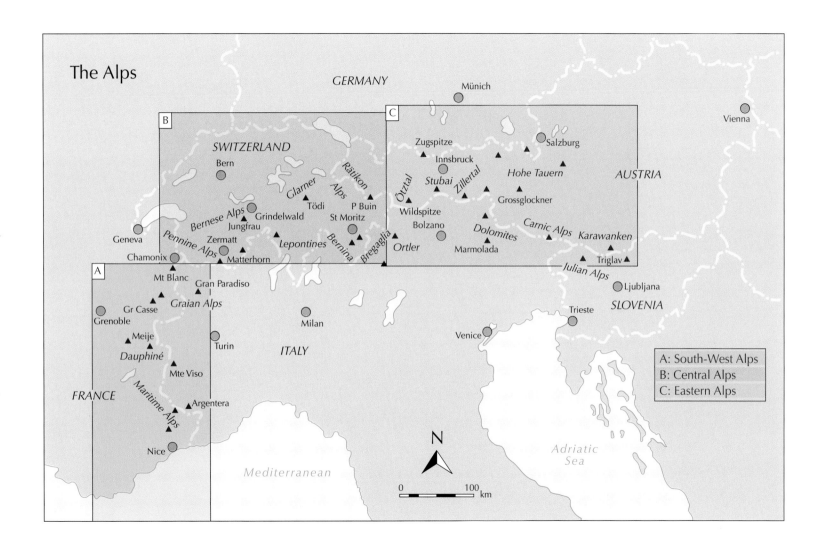

The Alps

GERMANY

Münich

Vienna

B

SWITZERLAND

Bern

C

Zugspitze

Salzburg

Innsbruck

AUSTRIA

Glarner

Rätikon

Alps

Tödi

P Buin

Stubai

Öztal

Hohe Tauern

Zillertal

Bernese Alps

Grindelwald

St Moritz

Wildspitze

Grossglockner

Carnic Alps

Jungfrau

Karawanken

Geneva

Pennine Alps

Zermatt

Lepontines

Bernina

Bregaglia

Bolzano

Dolomites

Triglav

Chamonix

Matterhorn

Ortler

Marmolada

A

Mt Blanc

Julian Alps

Ljubljana

Gran Paradiso

Graian Alps

SLOVENIA

Gr Casse

Trieste

Grenoble

Meije

Milan

Dauphiné

Turin

Venice

Mte Viso

ITALY

FRANCE

Maritime Alps

Argentera

A: South-West Alps
B: Central Alps
C: Eastern Alps

Nice

N

Adriatic
Sea

Mediterranean

0   100 km

km

Almost 40 years ago I went to the Alps and, like thousands before me, immediately fell under their spell. Driven by memories of that first visit, four months later I turned my back on a conventional nine-to-five existence, caught a train to Switzerland and found work among the snowbound mountains. In the decades since, I've returned almost every year – sometimes two or three times in a year – to walk, trek or climb, to lead walking groups, to work out routes for guidebooks or to do research for writing and photographic assignments. As a result, my loft now groans under the weight of research notes and route diaries, while my study contains many thousands of transparencies, from which I've selected the hundred or so images for this book to represent the Alpine chain as it stretches from the Maritime Alps to the Julians of Slovenia.

Scenically, the Alps have amazing diversity. There's a vast difference, for example, between the snowbound and glacier-hung peaks of the Pennine, Bernese and Dauphiné Alps, and the abrupt, eccentric pinnacles, towers and turrets of the Dolomites. The limestone features of the Rätikon Alps are very different to those of the Brenta, Tennengebirge and Julian Alps. And though shaped by the same cataclysmic forces that produced Mont Blanc and the Matterhorn, the rolling, grass-covered highlands at the heart of the Eastern Alps are in another league of visual drama, yet they have their own undeniable appeal and no shortage of admirers, and I've tried to represent that difference here.

I'm also at pains to stress that contrary to a popular misconception – in circulation since at least the late 19th century – the Alps are not yet overcrowded or finished. Some of my images and text hint at where, if desired, one can easily find solitude even in the height of summer. But I'm not going to give away all the secrets. There are some discoveries best made by your own efforts!

After several decades of activity, I've discovered that the best of the Alps is not reserved solely for the climber. The walker prepared to stray into distant valleys, exploring high alp pastures, moraine banks and remote passes and ridge crests, will find a world of infinite beauty waiting. To emphasize this belief, with one exception all the images in this book were taken within a few paces of a trail. My hope is that those of my readers who share my love of the Alps will be reminded of scenes that brought pleasure in the past, and that these will serve as a spur to fresh discoveries in the future.

Kev Reynolds

In the south-east corner of Switzerland, not far from the Italian border and 700 metres above the valley bed, the abrupt slope suddenly eases to a shelf of pasture, not level but rolling with hillocks and hollows, in one of which a pool mirrors distant peaks and glacial curtains. Up there above the chestnut woods, beyond roads and villages, beyond the reach of electricity and piped water, a handful of men and women spend their summers grazing cattle and making cheese in one of a row of timber-and-stone buildings snug against the next steep rise.

I've known this alp for almost 40 years. Many's the time I've puffed my way up the seemingly never-ending path that battles among clumps of wild raspberry and rosebay willowherb, and emerged from woodland at last to crest the final bluff with more than a smile of relief at the familiar vista spread before me.

I was there again a few weeks ago, at the tail end of a long, dry summer, to be confronted by a parade of ragged spire and shrinking icefield, pushed unbelievably high out of valleys whose depth could only be guessed. It shook me, as it always shakes me, with surprise – the surprise of the familiar that caught my breath and briefly moistened an eye.

Across the arterial valley that pushes into Italy, a tributary glen cuts into the wall of mountains directly opposite the alp of which I write, so that one's gaze penetrates right to its head. From shadow to sunshine, and from sub-tropical ferns and forest brushed with Lombardy's breath, that tributary leads the eye to abrupt granite fence-posts, slabs and snow-trimmed peaks – some of which carry the Italian border, while others divide one Swiss valley from another. There are blades of rock up there like bayonet spikes; stiletto spires and smooth-walled cirques tower over moraines formed by glaciers that no longer exist. On one of those moraines there's a mountain hut of the Swiss Alpine Club; another stands on a shelf of rock gained by a path of unrelenting steepness – the two being linked by as exciting a four-hour trek as you could possibly wish to tread.

All that was a backdrop, though; something on which to focus my gaze as, sprawling on the grass of the alp, I breathed the fragrance of sun-dried vegetation, strained my ears to the myriad sounds that townsfolk imagine to be silence, soaked up the view and reckoned – not for the first time this summer – that I'd found heaven.

Heaven in a View

To those of us who are drawn year by year to the mountains, who spend our winters reliving yesterday's scenes and anticipating tomorrow's, there really can be what seems like heaven in a view.

Long before our time John Ruskin, that Victorian arbiter of natural beauty who wandered the Alps during much of the Golden Age and became one of its most influential troubadours, claimed that mountains were 'the beginning and end of all natural scenery'. Were that all he had to say on the subject, we who are also smitten might applaud his opinion. But then we discover that, despite his great love of the Alps, in a fit of ill-judged discrimination he dismissed much that the mountains have to offer. 'All the best views of hills', he wrote, 'are at the bottom of them'.

At the bottom of them?

On the other hand some find satisfaction only in dramatic scenes of vertical rock or narrow crests of ice, and rejoice in the gymnastics that bought them that view. Exciting though they certainly are, to my mind summit or ridge-top views often lack one essential – the contrast of colour, tone and texture. True, the rock sometimes wears a palette of lichen; ice can fold into turquoise shadow; while snowfields soften blue or take on the blush of sunrise and sunset. But the basic ingredients are missing.

To make the view complete, to bring heaven to earth, so to speak, my preference is for a mid-mountain vantage point. Neither valley bed nor lofty summit, but somewhere in between, this point allows you to gauge both height and depth, to appreciate meadow and glacier, stand of pine and bare rockface; to look up and down in a single glance and absorb the best of both worlds. In short, alps upon the Alps.

The Overcrowded Alps

The Alpine chain rewards with innumerable magnificent viewpoints. From the rocky, tarn-spattered Maritime Alps above Nice to the Julians of Slovenia, the lover of fine scenery is spoilt for choice, and for two centuries and more Europe's premier mountain range has created dreams in the minds of all who turn to the high places for inspiration or adventure, and then answered those dreams in full measure.

That is one of its problems. The Alps have been too successful, too fulfilling, too scenically rewarding. Alpine tourism, which includes climbers, walkers and trekkers, as well as skiers and package tourists who arrive by the coachload, has for a long time been a major source of revenue whose influence can be partly blamed for changing and reshaping the Alpine environment – rarely, if ever, for the long-term good. The Victorian epithet 'The Playground of Europe' has never been more apt than it is today. But the tarmac of that playground, and its mechanical adornments, threaten to destroy the natural beauty that is its most appealing feature.

Not surprisingly, there are those who, having taken their fill, complain that the Alps are now finished, that they're overcrowded and tamed, that mass tourism has destroyed their original charm. Long ago Martin Conway, the distinguished mountaineer, art critic, writer and explorer, acknowledged such a gloomy attitude when he wrote that 'each generation makes of the world more or less the kind of place they dream it should be; and each when its day is done is often in a mood to regret the work of its own hands and to praise the conditions that obtained when it was young'.

Whilst admitting the concentration of skiers among specific resorts in winter, dozens of honeypot regions also attract climber, walker, trekker and general tourist in huge numbers during the relatively short mountain summer, effectively crowding the Alps from season to season. Yet this is a generalized view, a myopic misconception that's neither novel nor new.

Agreed, one would not expect to find solitude in Chamonix, Zermatt, Grindelwald or Selva; yet there is another side to the Alps, with no shortage of stunningly beautiful massifs where it's still possible to spend weeks of high summer in virtual seclusion. There are villages, populated year-round, whose only way of approach is along an ancient mule-track two hours' walk from the nearest road. Others snug among the mountains see no more than a handful of stray visitors from one summer to the next. There are alp hamlets untouched by modern technology, and scores of untrekked semi-wilderness areas in the very heart of Europe for those prepared to shun fashion and study the map.

Decades of Alpine wandering have opened my eyes to many of these special places and taught me that even in the most popular regions, at the height of summer, it's still possible to spend hours alone in the most amazing landscapes, their existence unguessed by the majority of visitors who continue to tread the known way. The pioneering spirit can still be satisfied in the 21st century. All one needs is an enquiring mind, a map and the ability to 'read' the country. Anyone who loves mountains for what they are, rather than what fashion, fame or notoriety have attached to them, and anyone who cares more for solitude than crowded familiarity, and for the little-known as well as for the famous, will find among the Alps more than enough to satisfy a lifetime of adventure.

Consider my alp, 700 metres above the valley which eases out of Switzerland and into Italy. On the numerous occasions I've been there, with a view to match any in the Alpine chain, I've not seen anyone other than the cheesemakers.

Overcrowded? Hardly.

Making the Connection

Mountains reward at different levels, for beauty in nature has many layers and languages with which to speak to us. It's quite possible to visit the Alps for the first time, ride to a summit by cable-car and gaze on a huge panorama with a very real sense of awe and wonder without recognizing a single feature in it. It's perfectly feasible to appreciate the scene at face value – without understanding why the landscape is the way it is; without any personal involvement in it; without connecting.

But imagine someone standing on that same summit who has previously journeyed through the landscape on foot. In making that journey he will have had an opportunity to build a relationship with the district and be able to recognize a variety of different elements in the summit view – a ridge, saddle or rockface, perhaps, or a certain valley, glacier or belt of forest. Personal experience will have added familiarity to the panorama, and although in essence the scene remains identical to the two viewers, their depth of appreciation will be very different.

But there are other layers of appreciation, too, revealed through degrees of understanding and perception. A geologist, for example, may view the landscape on a large scale, seeing in it immense convulsions that brought the Alps into being; sense the primeval forces of uplift and folding; and acknowledge the mountain's vulnerability as erosion by frost and rain bites away at its surface. He will know by instinct or by training whether the bedrock is limestone, sandstone or granite; will recall how pieces of that rock feel in his hand; know how quartz crystals dazzle in the sunlight.

By contrast the botanist may reduce that same panorama to a series of micro-landscapes and, revelling in his own field of specialism, identify specific habitats and soil types, and remark upon individual plants that clothe his mountains – the miniscule alpines on rockface and moraine bank, cushion plants embedded in scree, alpenroses flaming scarlet on acres of hillside, the dwarf pine scrabbling at the upper limit of the treeline.

Disciplines like these add another dimension to an appreciation of the view. Yet these can also be a distraction, for to concentrate on any one part of the landscape can detract from the rest.

To gain most from the mountain experience I believe one should retain a childlike sense of wonder for each segment of the natural environment and, where possible, refine the art of awareness; that is, strive to become conscious of each moment of being, and be sensitive to the world about you.

Attempting to reach that goal can be life enhancing. Once gained you can journey among the mountains liberated from distant concerns and allow the natural world to fully engage your senses. You will absorb like a sponge the rich kaleidoscope of sounds, scents and flavours that fill the air you breathe; delight at the play of light in mist, at cloud shadows that ripple across a distant hillside, at the moon drifting among stars in a sky unaffected by light pollution; revel in the brittle sound of frost forming on autumn grass.

The more intense each moment's experience, the greater will be your empathy and love for the natural world. By observation and awareness you will come to recognize the different rock types under foot and finger by their texture and colouring; appreciate lichens that stain both tree and boulder; and understand the truth that each tiny plant, insect, bird and granule of rock is as much an integral part of the Alpine environment as the mountains themselves.

By appreciating its fullness, by recognizing the myriad ingredients that make the complete picture, one builds a lasting relationship with the living, ever-evolving world. The landscape is then drawn into crisp focus; it becomes part of you, for you will have connected with it, and it is this connection that makes for spiritual uplift and gathers truth from a view.

✳ ✳ ✳

Reflections in the Alpenglow

The limestone wall of the Rätikon Alps softened in the slow, lingering dusk. Seated on the hut terrace, I was served my meal with finches chittering in a pine grove nearby. One flew to an upper cone, perched there, threw back its head and called to the dying sun. On this, my first visit to these mountains, I'd spent several days wandering alone over meadow, ridge and summit in an orgy of pleasure, and the finch's song echoed my contentment.

Shadows were swallowing screes when, meal over, I went for a stroll to ease muscles taut from a long day over rough ground. Across a neighbouring alp, then along a path under turrets catching the alpenglow, I turned a corner and came face to face with a tanned octagenarian in cord breeches with red braces, check shirt and Tyrolean felt hat, who looked as though he'd emerged from a 19th-century painting by E.T. Compton. His pale, watery eyes shone with pleasure, his leathery skin folded into innumerable creases, and a day's white stubble bristled his chin. 'Is this not the most wonderful of evenings?' he demanded in a breathless German dialect.

I agreed that it was, and for 10 minutes or so we shared a common delight at the slumbering mountains and their gullies, the valley, the chaos of boulders at the foot of the screes, the alpenroses, streams, a small green pool and the rim of dwarf pines that outlined a nearby moraine. He had known 60 or more Alpine summers in his 80-plus years, yet his enthusiasm was as fresh as that of a 16-year-old. It lit his features and bubbled from every pore, and I noticed, when we parted, a surprising spring to his step as though by sharing his love of life he'd been rejuvenated.

I was encouraged by our encounter, and by the knowledge that both he and I in our own fashion had experienced the wonder of the mountains in decades now gone, but could still celebrate the continuing glories of the Alps as they are today and be uplifted by them.

This collection of images is part of that celebration. It is a harvest of days well spent among one of the world's great mountain ranges, a selection and a reflection of Alpine points of view.

Pra Gra above Arolla, Pennine Alps

The true alps are not the mountains themselves, but the high pastures that for generations have been the destination of the transhumance. These, and the simple hamlets settled upon them, lend a human dimension to the landscape. With their stone-laid roofs and dark timber walls, the dairymen's chalets and small granaries of Pra Gra adorn a gentle slope of pasture an hour's walk above Arolla. Minor streams drain the slopes nearby, while marmots scuttle among the rocks and cowbells chime the hours. Across the valley Mont Collon is a great iced gateau of a peak, with its neighbour l'Evêque leaning away to its right. Climbing out of the picture on the far right a ridge slants up to the ever-popular Pigne d'Arolla, noted for its summit panorama. Forming part of the backbone of the Pennine Alps, these mountains are almost constantly on show to walkers exploring the fine network of paths that makes Arolla such a rewarding base for a holiday. Pra Gra simply adds to its appeal.

Vanoise flower meadow

Through the early summer months countless meadows right across the Alpine chain reward visitors with a bewildering display of flowers. Especially rich are those of the limestone ranges, as seen here in the heart of the Vanoise National Park of the Western Graian Alps, where the damp meadows explode into a riot of colour, fragrance and sound, as the warmth of the morning sun dries overnight dew and entices thousands of insects in the jungle of stems to serenade the day with an electric seething. Several varieties of vetch compete with the silky blue campanulas in this kaleidascope of colour; common plants, perhaps, but as dazzling to witness as the rarest orchid. Though a botanical background may add to one's interest, it's not a prerequisite for the enjoyment of the Alps in bloom. Flowers in the meadows and on moraine bank and rockface form an integral part of the mountain landscape, and without them the Alps would be much less powerful to the senses.

Dairyman at work on an alp

Life on some of the remote alps continues to revolve around traditional methods of farming based on the transhumance, as it has for many generations. In June, when the last of the snow has melted from the hillsides, and grass turns lush green after being drab and khaki-coloured following a long winter hidden from the sun, farmers leave their valley homes behind to lead their animals up onto the alps. For three months herds graze the high pastures, increasing their milk yield, which is then turned into cheese. Now, in the 21st century, dairymen still work long hours in their chalets over bubbling copper couldrons, cut off from a more conventional life-style and divorced from modern technology. In mid-September the summer is drawing to a close – alp hamlets are made ready for the coming winter; large, wheel-like cheeses are transported down to the valley; and cattle are brought down too in long, bell-clattering processions led by the prize cow adorned with a headdress of flowers and tufts of pine.

Alpine marmot *(Marmota marmota)*

No journey among the mountains in summer would be complete without sight or sound of that most endearing of Alpine creatures, the marmot, which brings life to the high alps and their rocky margins. Weighing as much as 10kg, and living in underground burrows or crevices among rocks for a six-month period of hibernation, this furry brown rodent mates almost as soon as he wakes in the springtime. Feeding on the lush grass and roots of high pasturelands, the young grow plump and store much-needed fat for the lean months – although some cubs are inevitably lost to a predatory fox or eagle, despite the famous warning 'whistle' emitted by an alert adult from the back of its throat. This shrill alarm call is often the first indication that marmots are nearby, although they may have been aware of your approach for some time. During the autumn, dried grasses are scythed by the adult's sharp, chisel-shaped teeth, then dragged down into the burrows to make nests for the coming winter.

Refuge de Vallonpierre, Écrins massif

Given sufficient time, money and energy, it would be possible to make a continuous tour along the entire Alpine chain from one end to the other, staying each night in a different hut. Many of these belong to the various national Alpine Clubs; others are privately owned but open to all-comers, and they vary in size, ambience and in the facilities on offer. Some are little more than basic shelters. Some are large, inn-like buildings with hot showers and twin-bedded rooms as well as communal dormitories, and are staffed throughout the summer by a guardian and his assistants who provide meals and refreshments of a standard similar to those of a resort hotel. Practically every mountain hut, however, enjoys a spectacular location, as suggested by Refuge de Vallonpierre, set beside a clear tarn high above the Valgaudémar in the Massif des Écrins. Owned by the Gap section of the French Alpine Club, the CAF, this is visited by trekkers tackling the 10–12 day Tour of the Oisans.

Snowpeak riding a cloud, Écrins massif

Clouds add much to the visual drama of the mountain scene – at one moment hiding, the next revealing, individual summits, crags or ridges. This snow-dashed peak, which overlooks La Bérarde in the heart of the Écrins district, has momentarily lost its roots and appears to drift across the valley. Autumn has arrived and there's a bite to the air. There are few visitors left and the huts are closed. Rain turns to sleet or snow that melts with the return of the sun – but for how much longer? Winter cannot be far away, and with each morning's dawn we study the clouds and gamble on what might be achieved. Sometimes we can smell snow in their drift and there's a chance we might be caught out should we go too high. Sometimes those clouds are below us, boiling up from lower valleys, sweeping our way, swallowing villages, hillsides and summits too. Then they're all around us and the world is lost, obscured by its clammy embrace – a compass needle the only truth in a hidden land.

Combin massif, Pennine Alps

The Combin massif is the first big block of mountains east of the Mont Blanc range, and from some angles it appears to mimic the Monarch of the Alps itself. Seen here from the balcony trail of the Sentier des Chamois, which teeters along abrupt slopes high above Val de Bagnes, an unobstructed view shows the highest of its summits – the distant shadowed peak of Combin de Grafeneire at 4314 metres – with the Glacier de Corbassière swirling below it. Standing on the glacier's right-hand lateral moraine, the Panossière hut, which makes a worthwhile destination for a day's walk from Fionnay, is used as the main base for climbs on this north side of the massif. Some consider the view from that hut to be the finest of the Grand Combin, but the vantage point gained by walkers on the Sentier des Chamois has the bonus of both height and distance by which to appreciate the full scale and complexity of the massif.

Pers glacier basin, Piz Palü, Bernina Alps

The sheer scale of the Alpine scene can be gauged in this view of the glacial basin below Piz Palü in the Bernina Alps, where a rope of six climbers makes its way down the Pers glacier after completing a traverse of the frontier ridge. Riven with crevasses, at this eastern end of the massif there is also an icefall to contend with, but the icy highway eventually leads to the Diavolezza restaurant which enjoys one of the most magnificent full-frontal mountain views in all the Alps. Since the Diavolezza can be reached by cable-car from the Val Bernina, it's invariably busy on bright days in both summer and winter. From it, walkers can reach the uncomplicated summit of Munt Pers, a tremendous 3207 metre lookout from which to study not only Piz Palü, with its triple-buttressed summits, but the lovely Bellavista crest, Piz Bernina, Piz Morteratsch and their long glacial tongues. That viewpoint, however, is a very different proposition from the one shown here.

Dents du Midi at sunset, Pennine Alps

With the onset of night, individual mountains lose their identity in a wash of shadow. From a point high above Val de Bagnes at the western end of the Pennine Alps, the Dents du Midi are profiled by the fast-fading light of sunset. This is a magical time to be in the Alps. Uplifted by a day well spent, and now seduced by a calm evening and a comforting forecast, a planned bivouac is something to look forward to. Or maybe you prefer the conviviality of a remote hut or perhaps a tent pitched far from habitation. At any rate, it is good to spend the night high above valleys and villages, where you can absorb a peace unique to the wild places of this earth, gather the darkness like a blanket and become lost in the crowded wonder of a night sky. There is no loneliness in such a night spent on one's own, of choice, for there's the mystery of dawn just a few short summer hours away. And another day to be lived to the full.

On their way to climb in the Dauphiné Alps in the early summer of 1864, Whymper, Moore and Horace Walker, together with their guides Almer and Croz, chose a point among the Aiguilles de la Saussaz north of La Grave from which to study the mountains they were about to visit. 'The view was one of the most gorgeous I ever saw', wrote Moore in *The Alps in 1864*, and then went on to enumerate the main features in that panorama. Of particular interest was La Meije, 'one of the finest walls of mingled crag and glacier in the Alps'. He noted that from this view the mountain had no distinct summit but a crown of many pinnacles. 'From the very top of the western peak', he continued, 'the ridge falls in a tremendous precipice to a remarkable narrow gap, beyond which it rises less steeply to the long shattered crest of the Râteau.' West of the Râteau lay the Col de la Lauze with 'the Glacier du Mont de Lans, which stretched away from it to the right for miles, a vast level field of névé. At the far end of this glacier, but some distance beyond it, a crowd of fine peaks were seen, of whose names, even, we were ignorant.'

This stupendous panorama is on show to trekkers following the Tour de l'Oisans across the high pastureland of the Plateau de Paris on the stage that leads from Bourg d'Oisans to La Grave, while a full-frontal view of La Meije is seen from the slopes above La Grave, where the string of hamlets known as the Hameau de Valfroide offers the first signs of habitation when coming down from the Aiguilles de la Saussaz. From here, as from several other vantage points above the Vallée de la Romanche, La Meije looks truly formidable and casts its personality over a wide area.

That same mountain is equally impressive when viewed from the south, on the approach through the Vallon des Etançons from La Bérarde.

As you draw closer to it, its southern face presents what seems to be a vertical wall, softened hardly at all by a mere fragment of glacier trapped high up, but with a napkin of ice at its foot, between wall and fan of scree. The wall is 800 metres high, measured from the Etançons glacier to the summit of the Grand Pic at 3982 metres, an awesome piece of mountain architecture which blocks the head of a wild, enchanted valley.

The Vallon des Etançons is a truly splendid valley, although surprisingly Whymper described it (in *Scrambles Amongst the Alps*) as 'a howling wilderness, the abomination of desolation … suggestive of chaos, but of little else'. Moore agreed: 'There was no end to it, and we became more savage at every step, unanimously agreeing that no power on earth would induce us to walk up or down this particular valley again.'

Then he relented. 'The scenery', he confessed, 'is, nevertheless … of the highest order of rugged grandeur.' But such could be said to describe virtually the whole of the Massif des Écrins, for this is one of the gems of the South-West Alps.

Parks to Protect the Mountains

It may come as a surprise to discover that large areas of the South-West Alps are among the least developed in the whole Alpine chain, despite the fact that both mountaineering and skiing activities have some of their most important centres here. But there's a world of difference between bustling Chamonix, Courmayeur or Val d'Isère and the huddled *communes* of the Écrins, Cottian or Maritime Alps, and there are marked contrasts of scale and visual drama between the Mont Blanc range and, say, the intimate cirques and chaotic high valleys of the

Mercantour. Yet it is this degree of diversity that invests the Alps with much of its appeal.

Breaking out of the Mediterranean behind Monaco and Nice, the Alps push north for almost 250 kilometres before arcing eastward across the head of Italy. At first, in the south, France bears the lion's share of the mountains, with a series of massifs building towards the Italian frontier, beyond which they fall sharply to the Piedmont plain and the River Po.

These South-West Alps contain the greatest collection of national parks in the whole Alpine chain: Mercantour, Écrins, Vanoise and the neighbouring Gran Paradiso in Italy, not to mention the Parc Regional du Queyras overlooked by Monte Viso on the Franco-Italian border. Each park has its own identity, its own unique form of scenic grandeur and geographic dimension, and together they have managed to restrict the spread of insensitive development which was threatening to destroy the intrinsic beauty of the French Alps.

For it is somewhat ironic that France, with its wonderful heritage of traditional mountain villages that grace valley and hillside alike, should so abuse parts of the Alps by creating a rash of purpose-built ski resorts that represent, if nothing else, a form of architectural vandalism and apparent disregard for landscape harmony. The 'white gold' of the ski industry has much to answer for, but fortunately the establishment of national and regional parks has managed to limit further damaging, large-scale mechanical intrusion in selected areas, and put a seal of protection on a comparatively untamed mountain environment and its wildlife.

The Maritime Alps

At the southernmost end of the chain rise the Maritime Alps, a large part of which enjoys the protection of the Parc National du Mercantour, the newest and probably least known of any national park in France. Characterized by deep, pine-clad valleys, high pastures, craggy ridges and dozens of small lakes, the Maritime Alps spread both sides of the international frontier. Though glacier-free, and without any summit reaching 3500 metres, the region is nonetheless full of wild charm – the stony upper valleys being among the roughest and most desolate of any in the Alps – with its highest peak located less than 50 kilometres from the coast.

The vegetation in the lower valleys is almost sub-tropical, and the climate generous to outdoor activity. Orange-roofed Provençal villages, with all the simple charm of the south, crowd abrupt conical hills on the way to the mountains, while below Mont Bégo in the Vallée des Merveilles, tens of thousands of Bronze Age rock carvings are to be found in a landscape cluttered with boulder-choked hollows and jade-green tarns, which attract a regular stream of visitors and make this the busiest of the valleys in the Mercantour national park. Elsewhere the rugged, confused topography of the Maritime Alps creates a truly challenging country for mountain treks, scrambles and rock climbs well away from public scrutiny.

Dauphiné Alps

Comprising the Cottian Alps, Queyras, Écrins and Vercors, the mountains of Dauphiné cover a large, complex area north of the Maritime Alps. The first of these groups, the Cottian Alps, includes the Parc Regional du Queyras, a mostly green, gentle upland district that bulges into Italy, along whose border the loftiest summits are gathered. With no major centre, and avoiding any serious ski development, this is an isolated, unspoilt region that favours the walker, scrambler and trekker, for a number of its summits are accessible to the hillwalker, while the Tour of the Queyras makes a circuit of the district in about two weeks. Across the border in Italy, Monte Viso casts its personality over a vast area.

The highest, and arguably the best, of the mountains of Dauphiné are grouped to the south-east of Grenoble, where the Massif des Écrins lies at the heart of France's largest national park. It also boasts the country's three highest mountains outside the Mont Blanc range: Barre des Écrins (4102m), La Meije (3982m) and Mont Pelvoux (3932m). On each of these, chapters in the history of alpinism have been written that include some of its most enigmatic characters and more controversial exploits. But apart from that, the Écrins region is at once defiantly spectacular and enticing – a great crescent of snowpeak, glacier and valley with undeniable appeal. More than 100 summits rise to well over 3000 metres, while in many valleys the bare rock walls are so steep as to deny lodging to any permanent snow or ice. Away from road and village the heartland valleys are as seemingly remote and uncharted as any in the French Alps, and rightly suggest a wonderland for the active walker; while the Tour de l'Oisans (GR54) makes a multi-day circuit of the mountains amounting to almost 200 kilometres in length. Though not coming anywhere near the Tour of Mont Blanc in popularity, it is a tougher proposition than the TMB, and with scenery to compete with any Alpine district.

The Graian Alps
Astride the international frontier the Graian Alps are divided between the mountains of Beaufortain and Vanoise in France, and Gran Paradiso in Italy. Both Western and Eastern Graians have their own national park,

with a shared boundary some 14 kilometres long, and together they make up the largest nature reserve in western Europe. The Parc National de la Vanoise was the first to be established in France, largely as a means of protecting the ibex, whose preservation was already assured in the neighbouring Gran Paradiso region thanks to protection afforded by the creation there of Italy's first national park in 1922.

The Graians are limestone mountains, heavily glaciated and snow-capped, with beautiful flower meadows, lakes, waterfalls and streams, their inner valleys dotted here and there with old mottled-stone farms, ruins and mountain huts patronized by walkers. On the periphery of the Vanoise park the close proximity of several heavily used ski resorts illustrates both the pressures and the successes of national park status, for only a short walk away from bulldozed pistes and a lacework of cableways is a haven of unmarked hillsides and hanging valleys alive with marmot, chamois and ibex.

And on both sides of the international border walkers' passes reveal scenes of great beauty to trekkers tackling the classic Tour of the Vanoise, the week-long Gran Traversata del Gran Paradiso or the Alta Via della Valle d'Aosta.

Long-distance walks aside, both Western and Eastern Graians are rich with walking opportunities, for a great number of paths have long been established there – in the 1880s, for example, some 350 kilometres of tracks were made in the Gran Paradiso region by Vittorio Emanuele II to further his hunting ambitions. Some of the hunting lodges and mountain huts built at the same time and for the same purpose have been adapted for present-day walkers and climbers, and on both sides of the frontier national park authorities have added to the number of simple lodgings, so the visitor is well catered for.

The Mont Blanc Range

For more than two centuries the highest mountain in western Europe has acted as a beacon to climber and non-climber alike. But Mont Blanc is much more than a lofty dome of snow and ice at 4807 metres, for as anyone who has gazed upon it will admit, the Monarch of the Alps has a wealth of consorts.

The range it surveys measures a little under 40 kilometres by 15, and is said to include some 400 summits and dozens of glaciers. Such a statistic can mean anything or nothing; what is important to the lover of fine scenery is that it represents the ultimate in visual drama. Viewed from almost any angle, there's something to catch your breath with wonder; be it a granite aiguille poking through a skein of mist, a river of ice projecting between rocky portals, or a crest of snow outlined against the deep blue Alpine sky, Mont Blanc rewards with a rich harvest of memorable scenes.

Happily it's not essential to be a climber to witness some of the best. Nor is it necessary to take mechanical aid to reach an outstanding viewpoint, for the modest walker is well served with trails on all sides of the range from which to experience the full gamut of scenic drama.

Best viewed at mid-height with a valley in between to create the perspective of scale, the panorama displayed from the slopes of the Aiguilles Rouges above Chamonix competes for top marks with the Italian flanks of Val Veni or Val Ferret on the southern side, while the eastern outliers are seen to perfection from one or two points high above the Swiss Val Ferret. Trekkers on the Tour of Mont Blanc, of course, are treated to a feast of visual delights.

The international appeal of Chamonix guarantees an almost permanent flow of visitors, but on the south side of the range Courmayeur is no poor second best. With an outlook as impressive as that of its more illustrious neighbour, this Italian centre has some stunning vantage points and no shortage of trails by which to reach them. Both centres provide countless opportunities for all forms of mountain-based sports, so it's no surprise to find that cableways devalue certain slopes above Courmayeur and Chamonix alike. In addition there's the renowned gondola lift that ferries visitors on an aerial traverse high above the Vallée Blanche from one side of the border to the other.

But for those who shun such aids and prefer to make their own way among the mountains, this is one of the most scenically rewarding districts in all Europe.

∗ ∗ ∗

Between Two Waters

In her gentle evocation of the Alps before the last war (*Mountain Holidays*), Janet Adam Smith tells how she came down the zigzags from the Col de la Vanoise in a thunderstorm and sought shelter at the old farmhouse of Entre deux Eaux, where she was made welcome by Madame Richard. The year was 1935, but her description of the building and its situation would be instantly recognized by anyone arriving there today.

The farmhouse, 'a stone chalet … long and low, rising at one end to a second storey', doubles as a refuge and stands precisely as the book suggests, at an Alpine crossroads in the heart of the Graian Alps within the Vanoise national park. To the north-east a trail curves into the seemingly barren, U-shaped Vallon de la Leisse, continues past another refuge owned by the national park authority, and crosses an easy saddle to the ski grounds of Tignes and Val Claret.

North-west of Entre deux Eaux lies the route to Pralognan via the Col de la Vanoise and Refuge Félix Faure under the west face of La Grande Casse. To the east the Vallon de la Rocheure is a flower-strewn glen at whose head (beyond Refuge de la Femma) there's a walker's col leading to Val d'Isère; while to the south of Entre deux Eaux the valley plunges into the Doron gorge.

Above the gorge on the west bank of the valley, across the way from Entre deux Eaux but more to the south-west, a gently tilted shelf of grass and stone carries the trail of GR5 below a series of cascades that drain the Glaciers de la Vanoise – the largest concentration of ice in the national park, spread across the Dent Parrachée, Pointe du Génépy, Dôme de l'Arpont and the Dôme de Chasseforêt. This section of GR5 has been adopted by the Tour of the Vanoise, seducing trekkers along that shelf and across its myriad streams among herds of ibex that roam in view of Refuge de l'Arpont, a three-hour walk from Entre deux Eaux.

Each of these trails is worth taking, for they nudge deeper into the Vanoise region – among marmot and chamois and banks of alpine flowers in the early summer. But there's another route, too, a short one of little more than an hour and a half; it heads south across the mouth of the Rocheure glen, dodges a narrow private road, meanders over pastures to the Chapelle St-Barthélémy, then sneaks past the Refuge du Plan du Lac and, 10 minutes later, reaches an idyllic tarn set in meadows at 2400 metres, high above the east bank of the Doron gorge.

Relaxing at the southern end of the lake, you become transfixed by one of the great views of the South-West Alps, for the solid wall of La Grande Casse, angling north-eastward to La Grande Motte, is cast before you as a mirror image. What appears to be the foremost summit (but is in fact the second highest), buttressed to a curving fin, is Pointe Mathews, named after William Mathews, one of the founding fathers of the Alpine Club, who made the first ascent in 1860 with his guide Michel Croz. The main summit stands back a little to the right of this, a ridge of snow cresting to it above the undetected Col des Grands Couloirs. That crest of snow is the culminating point of a glacier that spills down to the west to hang like a rumpled curtain over Lac Long.

The extensive wall of the Grande Casse descends obliquely to a low, dipping saddle before rising more sharply to La Grande Motte, which then disappears from view behind the black serrated rib of the Pointes de Pierre Brune. This rib becomes the dividing wall between the Vallons de la Rocheure and La Leisse, an upturned keel which also casts a reflection in the lake.

All this is captured and contained in a single glance. But there's more, for the westward view is also rewarding. One gains a hint (little more than that) of the hillside dropping beyond the Plan du Lac's containing grass hillocks into the Doron gorge, on the far side of which the Glaciers de la Vanoise engrave the horizon with a white outline and stipple the lake water as with an artist's brush.

Scenes like this underline the Alps' enduring appeal.

Lac de Trécolpas, Vallée du Boréon

Maritime Alps

The Parc National du Mercantour embraces a region of seemingly wild and remote mountains, the more surprising because of its proximity to the Mediterranean coast, whose influence is keenly felt in both climate and vegetation. Though considerably lower than neighbouring districts to the north, the Maritime Alps bear all the characteristics associated with larger mountains of the Alpine chain, save that of glaciers. Lakes are a distinguishing feature in many of the high valleys. Here, Lac de Trécolpas in the upper reaches of the Vallée du Boréon is one of the undisputed gems of the Mercantour park in the midst of country well suited to walkers who enjoy cross-country treks. Cradled within an arc of rocky peaks, and easily reached by a very pleasant walk of 1½ hours from the roadhead east of Le Boréon hamlet, it lies only 30 minutes away from Refuge de Cougourde. By crossing the Pas des Ladres above the lake, walkers can also gain the valley and hamlet of La Madone de Fenestre, which has a CAF refuge in the village square.

La Meije, from the hamlet of Les Hières

Dauphiné (Massif des Écrins)

At 3982 metres the rock peak of La Meije is one of the finest in the Massif des Écrins, and among the most respected in all the Alps. When he visited the district in 1864, Edward Whymper was impressed by what he could see of the mountain from La Grave, saying 'it could hardly be spoken of too highly. It is one of the finest road-views of the Alps ... But from La Grave one can no more appreciate the noble proportions and the towering height of the Meije, than understand the symmetry of the dome of St Paul's by gazing upon it from the churchyard. To see it fairly, one must be placed at a greater distance and at a greater height.' This prospect of the mountain soaring above the deep Vallée de la Romanche is gained from the hamlet of Les Hières, which provides both that greater distance and height. The obvious saddle below and to the right of the Grand Pic is the Brèche de la Meije, first crossed by Whymper's party on 23 June 1864.

Vallon des Étançons

Dauphiné (Massif des Écrins)

In *Scrambles Amongst the Alps* Whymper wrote disparagingly of the Étançons glen, describing it as a 'howling wilderness', but to my mind it is one of the grandest in the Dauphiné. Rising steadily above La Bérarde it cuts a deep swathe into the mountains, its west flank building to the Massif du Soreiller, and its east wall topped by a cluster of peaks mostly hidden from view by rocky shoulders and intruding spurs. At its head stands La Meije, its south face looming with a touch of menace over a shrinking glacial neckerchief, at once both intimidating and appealing – an obvious challenge to climbers with ambition. The path that entices into the valley is well made. At first among trees, grassy patches and flowers, the path then turns to scree, rocks and boulder-littered levels running with streams. Throughout, the grandeur of the scenery is of the highest order. This view is to the south from a point roughly midway between La Bérarde and the Refuge du Châtelleret. It's late autumn, and a dusting of snow brings the first hint of winter's approach.

Vallon de Bonne Pierre

Dauphiné (Massif des Écrins)

Draining into the Vallon des Étançons a little above La Bérarde, the Bonne Pierre tributary receives the melt of a shrinking glacier responsible in the past for scooping out a rocky cirque topped by the Roche Faurio and Dôme de Neige des Écrins (on the right). The latter, at 4015 metres, is a major satellite of France's highest summit outside the Mont Blanc massif. This Vallon de Bonne Pierre is short, steep and wildly romantic, and it was here that Whymper's party bivouacked on the night of 24 June 1864 prior to making the first ascent of the Barre des Écrins. A.W. Moore, who was with Whymper, wrote (in *The Alps in 1864*) that while they were arranging their bivouac, 'the mist that enveloped the glacier and surrounding peaks was becoming thinner; little bits of blue sky appeared [to reveal] one of the highest summits of Les Écrins'. He later commented that the right-hand wall seen here 'is one of the sheerest precipices in the Alps; neither glacier nor snow can find a resting-place on it'.

Dôme de Neige des Écrins

Dauphiné (Massif des Écrins)

This north-west aspect of the Dôme de Neige des Écrins, seen from the slopes of the Tête de la Maye, reveals the broken nature of the Bonne Pierre face and the various arêtes which, despite a cluster of individual gendarmes and aiguilles, do nothing to spoil its symmetry. Tête de la Maye is a wonderful viewpoint from which to study not only the Dôme de Neige but much of the heart of the Écrins district. Having spent time enjoying its 360° summit panorama I began to descend, and was negotiating one of the fixed-cable sections when I spied a lone figure approaching the grass shoulder below. Hoping to catch him silhouetted against the Bonne Pierre glacier, I swung down the chain and dropped to the path with just enough time to get one shot before he disappeared from view. What is not obvious from this angle is that the figure is on the edge of a 700 metre precipice, and the glacier at the foot of the Dôme de Neige is almost six kilometres distant.

Mont Gioberney

Dauphiné (Massif des Écrins)

Seen from the barrack-like Temple Écrins refuge, just 2½ hours' walk from La Bérarde, the heavily glaciated Mont Gioberney (3352m) stands guard over the upper Vallée du Vénéon. Though by no means one of the highest in the district, it is a massive mountain, usually climbed from the Refuge de la Pilatte which lies below it. This photograph was captured in a lull between storms during a summer spent researching a guidebook to the Écrins National Park. The weather was untypically dreadful most of the time, with almost daily storms of a ferocious nature. Twice in one week my tent was flooded off a campsite, but I managed to miss not a single day's activity – at some point during each day whilst out exploring there would be a brief respite, the sun would appear and the mountains and valleys then glistened. This image was snatched during one such window of opportunity. Despite the weather (or perhaps because of it) it proved to be one of the most rewarding of summers, and my enthusiasm for the region was enhanced.

Icefall on the Glacier Blanc

Dauphiné (Massif des Écrins)

After crossing a glacial torrent near the Pré de Madame Carle roadhead, about five kilometres upstream from Ailefroide, a well-made zigzag path works its way among ice-smoothed slabs to a boulderscape with a full-frontal view of the Glacier Blanc. The glacier curves in a frozen cascade from an unseen basin below the Barre des Écrins to dominate an uncompromisingly wild scene. Not surprisingly, this is an extremely popular vantage point, and it's invariably crowded with families, groups and individuals picnicking there on bright days in summer. From here the continuing path crosses a footbridge, curves towards the glacier, then climbs grit-covered ledges and slabs on the approach to the Refuge du Glacier Blanc for close views of the icefall and for a more distant prospect of the multi-peaked Mont Pelvoux. The refuge stands about 250 metres above the viewpoint seen here, but between the two there's a small tarn and the stone-built Refuge Tuckett, retained as a museum to the days of the pioneering mountaineers who opened up this corner of the Alpine chain.

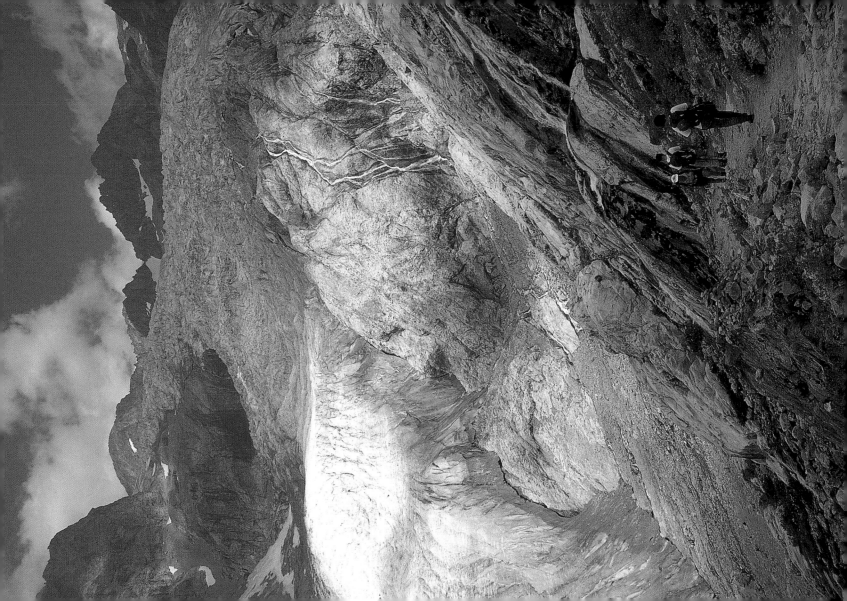

Glacier Noir

Dauphiné (Massif des Écrins)

Of the two glacier systems that spill towards the plain of Pré de Madame Carle at the head of the Vallée de la Vallouise, the more gently graded is that of the Glacier Noir, so-named because of the mass of dark-coloured rock debris that covers much of its ice. A trail teeters along the crest of the left-hand lateral moraine, from which a formidable wall consisting of rank upon rank of peaks that extend from Mont Pelvoux to l'Ailefroide can be studied at leisure. The crest is narrow and flower strewn, and in places the moraine has a tendency to crumble. But the path teases up to a large cairn built at about 2445 metres, then continues for another 60 metres or so under the Barre des Écrins, where you feel as though you've been drawn along an artery into the very heart of the mountains. From this point you look out on a panorama of rugged mountain architecture comprising rock slabs, hanging glaciers, screes, moraines and rubble-covered ice. It's a menacing, yet mesmerising scene.

Bosse de Clapouse, above Ailefroide

Dauphiné (Massif des Écrins)

Known mainly as a climbing centre, Ailefroide is little more than a small hamlet with extensive camping grounds set within a steep-walled valley. Nonetheless, it has no shortage of opportunities for the fit mountain walker. One of the more challenging of these is a fairly tough and full-day's outing which makes a direct crossing of the ridge wall that divides the Vallon de la Sélé from the valley of the Onde, by way of the 2799 metre Collet du Rascrouset. In its early stages the trail comes onto a scant, larch-topped bluff known as the Bosse de Clapouse, from where this photograph of Ailefroide's east flanking wall was taken. Six hundred metres above the valley, the bluff is an engaging place to spend an hour or two, especially when mists are drifting through the valley. Above and behind it the Vallon de Clapouse is a desolation of scree; but, just below, the stream which drains that scree falls in a riotous cascade of spray, adding something rather special to the approach walk.

Village scene, Bourg d'Arud

Dauphiné (Massif des Écrins)

Astride the road to La Bérarde in the Vallée du Vénéon, the unpretentious village of Bourg d'Arud is made bright in summer by troughs and pots of flowers placed outside some of the buildings. It's an uplifting scene which speaks of the local people's pride in their homes, and of their love of light and colour. Though only a small, modest village without any shops, Bourg does boast a couple of campsites, a *gîte d'étape* and two hotels, one of which is in the 17th-century Château de la Muzelle. South of the village a path climbs steeply through forest and over rough pasture to gain the Refuge de la Muzelle, which overlooks a lake of the same name and, to the south of that, a 2613 metre col crossed by trekkers on the Tour de l'Oisans. West of the refuge another trail negotiates a wild patch of country before dropping to the beautiful Lac Lauvitel, then continues down to La Danchère and returns to Bourg to complete a tough but rewarding circuit.

Col de la Muzelle

Dauphiné (Massif des Écrins)

Crossing the 2613 metre Col de la Muzelle between Valsenestre and Bourg d'Arud is usually the final challenge for trekkers working their way round the classic Tour de l'Oisans. From that col the view here is to the south after a day and a night of heavy rain. Down in Valsenestre morning had dawned grey, forbidding and wet, but as I gained height through the ravine-like glen and came to a narrow path struggling up a cone of shifting black shale and grit, so I broke through the cloud layer to be blessed by sunshine. Looking back across the cloud-sea I was delighted to find exposed in the middle distance the obvious saddle of the Col de Côte Belle, crossed on the previous stage. Beyond that I could believe those distant clouds were damping the hamlet of Le Désert in the little Valjouffrey, and tried to identify Col de la Vaurze that had led me there. However, looking north from Col de la Muzelle there were no clouds, just the promise of unbroken sunshine for the rest of the day.

Lac des Vaches and La Grande Casse

Graian Alps (Vanoise)

High above Pralognan the shallow Lac des Vaches lies trapped among moraine troughs below the south-west face of the Grande Casse. A causeway of stone slabs carries a pathway across the lake, which here is still partially frozen and dressed with snow in mid-July following a severe winter. From this point, one's attention is directed into the snowy basin of La Grande Casse, which gives birth to the Glacier des Grands Couloirs, now withdrawing into the cirque it has created. Once across the lake the route climbs among moraines below that glacier before curving round the Aiguille de la Vanoise to gain the surprisingly long, broad saddle of Col de la Vanoise, on which there is a CAF refuge. This is an extremely popular route for walkers staying in Pralognan, but it's also used (in the opposite direction) by trekkers working their way round the multi-day Tour of the Vanoise. Much of this region of mountains and lakes is contained within the Parc National de la Vanoise, whose network of hiking trails and mountain refuges provides numerous opportunities for hut-to-hut touring.

Plan du Lac

Graian Alps (Vanoise)

On a grassy shelf several hundred metres above the Doron gorge, this idyllic tarn spreads across the Plan du Lac to reflect the tranquillity of a summer's morning in which only the gentlest of breezes disturbs the water. The peak at far left is Pointe Mathews, named after one of the founding fathers of the Alpine Club. The main summit of La Grande Casse – highest in the Vanoise region at 3855 metres, and which Mathews climbed in 1860 – is the snow dome to the right of that. Then comes the long wall that extends eastward, finally rising to La Grande Motte (3653m). The dark prow of mountain that partially conceals the latter peak effectively divides the Vallon de la Rocheure from the Vallon de la Leisse. There's no shortage of refuge accommodation in the neighbourhood, the nearest being a short walk away to the north of the lake, where the PNV-owned Refuge du Plan du Lac serves as a comfortable base from which to explore several nearby valleys.

Vallon de la Rocheure

Graian Alps (Vanoise)

In the very heart of the Parc National de la Vanoise of the Western Graian Alps, the Vallon de la Rocheure is a major tributary of the Doron, whose waters in turn feed the Maurienne. The Rocheure is a gentle, pastoral valley, its meadows starred with flowers in the early weeks of summer. Marmot, chamois and ibex may all be found here enjoying the protection afforded by the park, while old stone buildings, weathered by a hundred winter storms and as many summer downpours, settle comfortably in the meadows and add to, rather than detract from the landscape. Near the head of the valley, Refuge de la Femma is a modern hut which acts as a springboard from which to set out for the Col de la Rocheure or to climb several local peaks, among them the Pointe de Méan Martin and Pointes du Châtelard. This image, however, is taken in the opposite direction, looking downvalley towards the west where mountains carry the Glaciers de la Vanoise. Cloud shadows darken slopes that tilt into the upper Doron gorge.

Grande Ciamarella and l'Albaron

Graian Alps (Vanoise)

Seen across the depths of the Haute Maurienne, a great sweep of snowfield and glacier adds to the visual appeal of the Ciamarella-Albaron massif, which carries the Franco-Italian border along its crest. The scene was captured from the Tour of the Vanoise, on a day that began in Bonneval at the foot of l'Albaron, then followed the GR5 north towards the Col de l'Iseran – but well away from the road. We found ourselves pausing often to enjoy a backward vision of that block of mountains which forms a link between the Western Graians of the Vanoise and the Eastern Graians that extend into the Gran Paradiso national park across the border. The prominent peak on the left is the 3676 metre Grande Ciamarella, while at the right-hand end of the glaciers l'Albaron is just 40 metres lower. Note the col in the extreme left of the picture; this is Col de Sea (3094m), which suggests a way over the mountains to Italy. Of such sightings are dreams made. And we who love mountains are, of course, incurable dreamers.

Herbétet-Paradiso massif

Graian Alps (Gran Paradiso)

Forming an icy divide between the Val Savarenche and Valnontey in Italy's Gran Paradiso national park, a lofty ridge extends northward from the Gran Paradiso itself to the graceful Herbétet, and continues from there to the Gran Serra. Glaciers adorn both the east and west flanks, and a very fine path tacks along the west slope – from where this photograph was taken – for about six kilometres to link the Vittorio Emanuele and Frédérico Chabod huts. The high mountains are concealed from view for part of the way, then suddenly you turn a spur to be confronted by glaciers, snow slopes and a wilderness of moraine debris. Since the national park was formed in order to protect the ibex, it's no surprise that both ibex and chamois can often be seen grazing or roaming without concern above the path, which adds to its many attractions. Standing below the shapely Herbétet, Rifugio Chabod is more modern than the Emanuele hut, and enjoys an open aspect looking up to the Montandayne glacier.

Lago de Lauson

Graian Alps (Gran Paradiso)

One of the most important valleys in the Gran Paradiso national park is Val di Cogne, which lies south of Aosta. But the finest scenery is to be found in and around its Valnontey tributary – a valley rimmed with shapely peaks and plastered with glaciers. Rifugio Vittorio Sella is well placed as a base for exploratory hikes here, as well as for viewing wildlife, and a 30 minute walk south of the hut leads to Lago de Lauson, a small tarn used as a watering hole by ibex. At the head of the valley the Tribolazione glacier hangs below a watershed ridge running from Gran Paradiso to the Tour du Grand St Pierre, and forms part of a dramatic cirque that lures walkers along a trail that traces the valley's west flank. Though narrow and moderately exposed at times, the path is well made, with several panoramic viewpoints that demand long moments of contemplation. In such places the sound of cascading streams and the odd clatter of a stone dislodged by an animal are all that disturb the peace.

Mont Blanc from Col de la Seigne

Mont Blanc

Viewed from the 2516 metre Col de la Seigne on the Franco-Italian border, Mont Blanc appears to be guarded by the twin Pyramides Calcaires, in the right foreground, and the Aiguille Noire de Peuterey, which appears through the saddle that divides them. This is the scene that greets trekkers on the renowned Tour of Mont Blanc after labouring up eroded slopes from the Vallée des Glaciers. Arrival at the col is a revelation, for a new world opens before you. Directly ahead a patched hillside falls away into the Vallon de la Lée Blanche, and, below, the Pyramides Calcaires slips easily into the Val Veni. Off to the right a maze of peak and ridge folds towards the Gran Paradiso and Eastern Graian Alps. But it is Mont Blanc, the Monarch of the Alps with its generous dome of snow and ice, that rightly demands – and receives – your full attention. Used by the Roman legions on their way into Gaul, this historic col is perhaps the most scenically rewarding of all those crossed by the TMB.

The balcony trail above Val Veni

Mont Blanc

Carrying most of their needs on their backs, three trekkers take the steeply climbing path that leaves the Vallée de la Lée Blanche by Lac Combal in order to work their way onto a balcony trail that runs along the south side of Val Veni, some 300 metres or so above the pastures. Adopted by the Tour of Mont Blanc as one of the approach route options that lead to Courmayeur, the stage usually begins at Rifugio Elisabetta Soldini, built on a spur extending from one of the Pyramides Calcaires. After an easy start to the day reality sets in as you leave Lac Combal, for the trail now slants uphill, passes a few ruins and abandoned alp buildings, crosses streams and labours up sharply angled grass slopes. In a little over an hour from the lake the way reaches a high point of 2430 metres. Views are uplifting throughout, and the sharp, needle-like peak of the Aiguille Noire, seen here piercing the clouds, gives an indication of the visual pleasures to come.

Aiguille de Tré la Tête

Mont Blanc

Almost every district of the Alpine chain has its balcony trails from which extraordinary views can be won of the surrounding mountains. The Mont Blanc range is no exception to this, and on the north and south sides of the massif high paths provide spectacular vantage points from which to study the mountains across intervening valleys that provide the essential perspective of distance. That which picks a route along an undulating shelf above Val Veni on the Italian slope is a particular favourite, celebrated by thousands of trekkers each summer. Near its western end a shallow pool lies in a saucer of flower-starred turf, turning the Aiguille de Tré la Tête on its head. On its left we see the sprawling Glacier de la Lée Blanche (or Lex Blanche as it's also known), while to the right the Miage glacier extends valleywards as a rubble-covered highway of ice. The summit crown of Mont Blanc is being dusted with cloud on the very right-hand edge of the picture, while the Glacier du Mont Blanc spills onto that of the Miage.

Reflections of Mont Blanc

Mont Blanc

Tackling a multi-day trek is the ultimate way to appreciate the geography of a region, for as the route journeys across ridge spurs and passes, delves into valleys and adopts high trails, the landscape is spread out in all its glory. Being a circular route, the Tour of Mont Blanc unveils the best of all sides of the range, so the trekker views not only its well-known face from above Chamonix, but the less-publicized – but by no means less spectacularly beautiful – Swiss and Italian flanks too. The balcony path above Val Veni west of Courmayeur is especially rewarding, for the south side of Mont Blanc also has its attendant aiguilles and glaciers protruding between them, mirrored in a series of small tarns and pools beside the trail. The drift of innocent clouds adds to the beauty of the scene, for there's a constant sense of expectation that any moment now a stray breeze will move them along to reveal Mont Blanc's snow dome, a ragged aiguille or the top of a precipitous wall of granite.

Col de Voza and the Chamonix Aiguilles

Mont Blanc

The lower end of the Chamonix valley is almost closed off by a long, arthritic ridge spur extending north-west and north from the Aiguille de Goûter, thus providing a number of vantage points from which to study the valley and its line of walling aiguilles. Col de la Forclaz, at its northern end, and Col de Voza, midway between St-Gervais and the aiguille, are the two main crossing points for walkers, while cableways and the Tramway du Mont Blanc which creeps along the ridge provide means of access to these viewpoints for less active visitors. For the majority of trekkers on the Tour of Mont Blanc who began their circuit at Les Houches, the crossing of Col de Voza is the first challenge. This 1653 metre col is reached in about 2½ hours, and from it one enjoys a splendid overview of the Vallée de l'Arve. While the TMB crosses the ridge here, other paths stray along the crest to extend and rearrange the view.

Grands Charmoz above Montenvers

Mont Blanc

Since 1908 a rack-railway has enabled hundreds of thousands of Chamonix visitors to enjoy the icy spectacle of the Mer de Glace from Montenvers. Crowds inevitably gather there, but it's not difficult to escape them by taking an extremely scenic path that swings above the station and its hotel and soon leaves all sign of buildings behind. Paved with slabs for some of the way, this path climbs nearly 300 metres among slopes of dwarf pine and alpenrose to gain a famed viewpoint known locally as the Signal (or Signal Forbes) at 2198 metres. Whichever direction your gaze takes on the approach to the Signal, tremendous walls and turrets of granite soar above the glacier, among them the Aiguilles Drus, Verte and Moine, Grandes Jorasses and, as seen here on the true right bank, the Aiguille des Grands Charmoz, which dwarfs the walkers seen near the foot of the picture. To the right of the Charmoz, a fluff of morning cloud obscures the impact of the Aiguille de Blaitière.

The Drus from Les Praz

Mont Blanc

Despite their immense height, Mont Blanc and its aiguilles can be admired from a number of places in the valley itself without appearing to be foreshortened. From the main square in Chamonix, for example, the very summit of Mont Blanc can be seen from restaurant tables, while on a short walk upvalley on the way to Argentière this impressive view of the Aiguilles Verte and Drus is revealed through the gap in the mountain wall created by the Mer de Glace. Flanked by the Verte, the granite obelisk of the Drus is a masterpiece of architecture, its north and west faces being an obvious challenge to climbers, while the shattered arête of the Flammes de Pierre creates a monstrous sawblade to its right. Les Praz de Chamonix offers one of the best views of the Drus – the snout of the Mer de Glace which lies below it being concealed by converging spurs and patches of forest. Behind Les Praz a cableway swings up to La Flégère for an equally fine view, but from a slightly different perspective.

Aiguilles Verte and Drus

Mont Blanc

In this picture, taken with a tele-lens from the 2191 metre Col de Balme, an unexpected dump of summer snow has transformed the Aiguilles Verte and Drus with a wintry garb. The bulky Verte is one of the most challenging of the '4000ers' prized among alpinists, while the Drus (on the right and looking very different here from the popular spear-like shape that it presents above Montenvers) also boasts some fierce routes and claims a proud climbing history. As for the Col de Balme, from which the photo was captured, this is one of the great Alpine viewpoints, known to thousands of trekkers working their way round the Tour of Mont Blanc. Situated at the upper end of the Chamonix valley, with the Franco-Swiss border drawn across it, Col de Balme commands virtually the whole valley and its flanking aiguilles, as well as the gleaming dome of Mont Blanc itself. Baedeker called it 'a superb view', while that Alpine connoisseur R.L.G. Irving claimed that 'If that view does not thrill you, you are better away from the Alps.'

Mont Blanc from the Grand Balcon Sud

Mont Blanc

The Grand Balcon Sud is a justifiably popular trail that winds at mid-height along the east flank of the Aiguilles Rouges, presenting to the walker and lover of fine scenery some of the most stimulating panoramic views of the Mont Blanc range. Though cableways elsewhere may insult nature's harmony, this bluff of grass and rock creates a balcony of delight. Gazing across the valley there is nothing to interrupt your field of vision. Directly in front, the hillside plunges in an abrupt sweep of grass, rock and forest to the Arve; above and behind, a few small lakes increase the enchantment; then there are scree tips that explode with slab, rib and pinnacle. But between the rumpled shelf that carries this trail and the sublime presence of Mont Blanc opposite, an airy sense of space provides the perspective of distance that affords scale to each view. Breaking away from the Grand Balcon, these walkers have gained a favoured vantage point from which to absorb the regal splendour of the Monarch of the Alps at its very best.

There's a valley wedged deep within the Lepontine Alps, cramped between granite walls that threaten to block out the sky, where lush green woods of beech, linden and chestnut trees edge stream and meadow. In this valley a small grey village appears to have grown out of the soil on a far-distant day of rain and sunshine, rather than to owe its existence to architects and builders. It's not much of a village, size-wise; just a collection of weathered dwellings and a few granaries at its fringe. Flat stone slabs overlap on rooftops, one blending against another in a huddled maze whose symmetry is broken only by the tall, thin tower of its church.

Behind the village a waterfall pours in a solitary spout from a strip of rock bordered by trees, its lip suggestive of a hanging valley hidden from view. Up there, somewhere out of sight, a forgotten stream feeds that cascade.

That hanging valley, like so many valleys in the Lepontines, is barely trod by the visitor in search of exercise and what Octavia Hill called 'the healing gift of space'. It's semi-deserted, littered towards its head by the ruins of an abandoned farm or two, whose time-smoothed stones are being swallowed by a rampant vegetation. The stream runs clear as glass to one side. Born among tarns a thousand metres up in the bald grey mountains, it sprays diamonds to the sun, but rests in green pools lower down among boulders big as houses.

Walking in that hidden valley is to experience the Alps of the first mountaineers. There are no flag-flying restaurants to heal a thirst with cold beer, no signposts or waymarks, no mountain hut serviced by helicopter. Nothing but raw nature and a wilderness of stone.

Other Lepontine valleys seduce with their promise of seclusion. I've bathed in their pools and, lying out afterwards, have been visited by butterflies that landed on sun-warmed arms and chests. I've climbed above lakes to traverse cols untouched by the waymarker's brush, and made circuits of snow-free massifs as rugged and trackless as on the day of their genesis.

Far to the north of the Lepontines, over many a long day's hike across mountains that wear glaciers, among limestone ranges unknown to the pages of tourist brochures and adventure magazines, and where villages have yet to become resorts, more valleys, alp hamlets and bristling crags in the very heart of Switzerland remain to be 'discovered'.

The Central Alps, as far as this selection of photographs is concerned, include all the mountains of Switzerland (apart from the pre-Alpine range of the Jura), the Italian flank of the Pennine, Lepontine and Bernina Alps, and Austrian borderlands of the Rätikon and Silvretta Alps. Though they may claim some of the most dramatic scenery and best-known mountains, with several of the busiest, most sophisticated and best equipped resorts in all Europe, it only takes a little planning to find a barely touched wonderland far from the gathering crowds.

The Pennine Alps

For those who seek what may be termed the quintessential Alps, much of the Pennine chain has a continued appeal that not even a century and a half of devotion has begun to erode. Since a fair daub of snow and ice appears to claim importance in the scenic scheme of things, it's no surprise that the mountains of canton Valais and its Italian counterpart are among the most appealing of all. Consider their pedigree: Matterhorn, Monte Rosa, Ober Gabelhorn, Weisshorn, Dom, Dent Blanche and Grand Combin, to name but a few. Their snowfields gleam far off, while their glaciers tumble and swirl and stretch out above green pastures to dramatic effect.

Running eastward from Col Ferret to the Simplon pass, the Pennine chain contains Europe's greatest collection of 4000 metre peaks west of the Caucasus. Most of these carry the Swiss-Italian frontier along a watershed of ice and snow interrupted by summits of striking individuality. From that crest transverse ridges push roughly north and south, from which outlying peaks project their own personality. Between them tongues of ice drain into long valleys; those to the north spill into the Rhône, while those on the Italian slope make complex journeys down to the Po.

A few of the valleys have been at the forefront of Alpine tourism since the mid-19th century, which saw the drama of mountaineering's Golden Age take place here. Others developed more slowly, while some (a handful) assume a welcome reluctance to change. Compare, for example, the upper Mattertal around Zermatt with the 'lost world' appeal of the Turtmanntal nearby or the apparent indifference to tourism experienced in the Arolla stem of Val d'Hérens. Visit the inner recesses of Val de Bagnes, tributary glens of the Saastal, or the upper Val Ferret under the frontiers of Switzerland and Italy, and you'll find a sense of remoteness unknown to those for whom the Matterhorn is the only mountain to see.

Of course, that huge arc of 4000 metre peaks that stretches either side of the Matterhorn is uncontestably one of the greatest sights of the Alpine chain, but other valleys enjoy scenes of extraordinary grandeur too, yet have never become one of the major tourist hot-spots. I think of the Val d'Anniviers, whose upper reaches are dwarfed by Weisshorn, Zinal Rothorn, Ober Gabelhorn, Dent Blanche and Grand Cornier. From some of the trails that creep beneath them, cross neighbouring hillsides or labour up intervening spurs, those mountains take on a Himalayan scale. With such a formidable backdrop, the walking potential is vast – mostly strenuous, maybe, but so very rewarding.

The Lepontine Alps

Also known as the Alps of Ticino, after the pear-shaped canton that projects south of the watershed into Lombardy, the mountains and secretive upper valleys of the Lepontines remain little-known to all but the aficionado. By contrast the sparkling lakeside resorts of Lugano and Locarno with their palm trees and neat formal gardens have about them an air of the Riviera.

The great Victorian mountain explorer D.W. Freshfield wrote about the district in rapturous terms, but few British writers since have been drawn to it (half a century ago J. Hubert Walker was an exception). There are no outstanding peaks with famous names, no test-piece climbs nor renowned multi-day treks, but as Walker pointed out, 'there is no single district of the whole Alpine chain better suited to a continuous walking-tour from valley to valley, from glen to glen, and there is scarcely a mountain in it whose summit cannot be reached by a rough uphill walk' (*Walking in the Alps*).

Monte Leone, rising above the Simplon pass, is the first and highest at 3553 metres. But although several others have undoubted appeal, it's not so much individual mountains that attract as the quality of the landscape in general – the tangled glens, unsophisticated villages, rocky high plateaus gemmed with lakes, remote alps, the ruins that tell of long-departed farmsteads, ancient hump-backed bridges, water-polished boulders and some of the clearest mountain streams to be found anywhere.

Writing of Val Bavona in the heart of the region, Freshfield said, 'in this valley the strength of granite is clothed with the grace of southern foliage, in a rich mantle of chestnuts and beeches, fringed with maize and vines, and embroidered about the skirts with delicate traceries of ferns and cyclamen. Nature seems here to have hit the mark she so often misses … in her higher efforts' (*Italian Alps*).

It's true that since Freshfield roamed these mountains, the hydro-engineer has had his day in one or two massifs, and Valle Leventina – the valley of the Ticino river that forms the district's main artery – has been sacrificed to trans-Alpine traffic, a major railway and a through-route for power lines. But these are the exceptions. By far the larger part remains unspoiled, challenging and richly rewarding to explore.

While the St Gotthard pass heads Valle Leventina, the Luckmanier (or Passo del Lucomagno) carries traffic over the mountains in the eastern half of the Lepontines, then down through Valle di Blenio. This is much quieter than the Leventina, and offers side glens, high terraces, a few mountain huts and several walkers' passes that could so easily be linked to form multi-day tours.

But the western half of the district has the largest number of inner glens and some of the highest peaks, jutting from an upthrust core of granite. Here it is the Valle Maggia that holds the key to discovery.

Approached from Locarno, Valle Maggia is flat and broad-bottomed at first, with a Mediterranean warmth and an atmosphere that is anything but Alpine, yet as it draws you slowly into the mountains, so the unique appeal of the district is introduced. At Cevio the valley forks, going west to the Vals di Campo and Bosco. In the latter valley, Bosco-

Gurin is the highest Ticino village, yet it has a closer affinity with canton Valais than any of these Italian-flavoured valleys.

The upper stem of Valle Maggia breaks again at Bignasco, and divides between the wonderfully romantic Val Bavona and Val Lavizzara, both of which lead up to the innermost granitelands of the Cristallina massif – a contorted landscape of grey rock and water where mists swirl in the evening, haunted by stray chamois that drift almost soundlessly among the ice-smoothed crags and boulders, a world away from the palm-fringed shores of Lago Maggiore.

Bernina-Bregaglia

The south-eastern corner of Switzerland not only pokes fingers into Italy but also shares a border with Austria. That long trench of a valley, the Engadine, cuts right through the region with the help of Val Bregaglia and Val Poschiavo. Bregaglia and Poschiavo bear all the hallmarks of the Italian Alps – the Upper Engadine, from Maloja to St Moritz, is an almost continuous sheet of water at around 1800 metres; while the Lower Engadine, with its forested slopes, sunny terrace, enticing side glens and sgraffiti-patterned villages, is lyrically Romansch in language, architecture and culture.

Flanking the Lower Engadine to the north rise the Albula and Silvretta Alps, while much of its south side is included within Switzerland's only national park, whose guiding principals are among the purest in terms of nature conservation of any such park in the world. Most of the inner valleys are heavily wooded, and as visitors are limited to where they can go – in deference to the indigenous wildlife – much of the district remains in a pristine condition. There is no tourist infrastructure apart from the Blockhaus Cluozza, which allows walkers to stay overnight inside the park; but there are other huts, inns and hotels on the outskirts from which to make expeditions in search of deer, chamois, marmot or ibex.

No peaks within the national park's boundaries have permanent snowfields or glaciers, but a short distance to the south mountains of true Alpine stature can be found. Here, gathered in a compact snowy mass just south of the confluence of Engadine and Val Bregaglia in view of Pontresina, the Bernina Alps take their name from the easternmost 4000 metre peak of the Alpine chain, which overlooks the Vals Roseg and Morteratsch. Its ridges stretch out to embrace a panoply of glorious snow mountains, among them Piz Roseg, La Sella and its neighbours at the head of Val Roseg, the immense spread of Bellavista, and the triple-buttressed Piz Palü. The latter, which gives birth to a major glacier system, would stand out in any mountain crowd for its bold lines, its symmetry and grace of form.

Separated from the Bernina group by the Muretto pass and Italian Val Malenco, the Bregaglia Alps have produced a district full of abrupt granite peaks, slabs and needles that pay homage to the singularly impressive Monte Disgrazia, which looks across to the south side of the Bernina and commands the wildly romantic Valle di Mello and the Preda Rosso basin. To be drawn into the rock-strewn valleys of the Bregaglia, or up onto its higher alps, is to experience mountain architecture at its very best in the most enchanted of settings.

These inner glens of the Italian Bregaglia, approached from the low-lying, wine-producing district of Valtellina by way of the narrow, rocky Val Masino, have gained a reputation among climbers for the severity of their granite cliffs; this is especially true of Valle di Mello. But one need not be a climber to be attracted to the charms of this Alpine back-of-beyond, for the rough paths that keep company with the stream that dallies here and there in pools shaded by birch and alder lead to a string of old farmsteads and a huddle of once-deserted buildings given a new lease of life. Sunlight beams through an avenue of granite, and if you travel far enough and clamber high enough, you'll gain a new and sudden vista of Monte Disgrazia. Catch it stained by the alpenglow, and the vision will remain with you always.

Then there's the Swiss Bregaglia falling in spirals from the Maloja pass, cleft on its southern side by the Vals Albigna and Bondasca, while a third glen, Val Forno, with its long glacial highway, hides behind the Albigna headwall and is best approached from Maloja itself.

On the steep north slope of Val Bregaglia stands the wonderful village of Soglio, described by the painter Giovanni Segantini as being on 'the threshold of paradise'. Above it remote alp hamlets bask in the sunshine and gaze across the valley to scenes of near perfection. Meanwhile, down in the bed of Bregaglia, luxurious chestnut woods fill the gaps between thick-walled villages crowded around cobbled squares.

The Bernese Alps

The year-round appeal of Grindelwald, Wengen and Mürren has effectively elevated the Bernese Oberland (the north-facing mountains east of the Lötschenpass) into the premier league of tourist invasion. In winter their slopes are among the busiest; in summer their streets, cableways and funiculars are patronized by tourists from around the world. Viewpoints such as Kleine Scheidegg, the Faulhorn, Bachalpsee and Männlichen rattle with the sound of camera shutters, while the Schilthorn and Jungfrau Joch annually reward tens of thousands of visitors with high mountain vistas previously unknown to all but active mountaineers.

One might be forgiven for thinking there is no escape, but that would be wrong, for a short walk from the crowd-rimmed Bachalpsee leads to a brace of tarns in an untamed landscape of scree and boulder. There's an accessible walkers' summit with a panorama to match that of the Faulhorn's, and a ridge to cross with fixed ropes for security on a steep descent that unwraps a view guaranteed to pull you up short with surprise.

Between the cable-strung Schilthorn, above Mürren, and the head of the Lauterbrunnen valley, a high ridge accessible by footpath provides a grandstand of jaw-dropping splendour, and at the foot of the valley's headwall a swirl of glaciers and old moraines excites with a true sense of wilderness. There are no crowds here.

Numerous side valleys, moraine trails, ridge systems and passes throughout the Bernese Alps can be enjoyed in peace, whether on the north or south flank, and the scenery is of the highest order almost everywhere.

It's not just the fabled triptych of Eiger, Mönch and Jungfrau, or the crenellated summit of the Wetterhorn, that adds glamour to a view of the Bernese Alps, no matter how many calenders and chocolate boxes are decorated with them. Schreckhorn and needle-pointed Finsteraarhorn are also part of Grindelwald's backdrop; the extraordinary ridge of the Gspaltenhorn is one of Mürren's prime attractions; Blümlisalp does much for Kandersteg when viewed from the Oeschinensee and above. Also part of the jigsaw are the Wildstrubel from Adelboden, the Wildhorn from Lauenen, Bietschhorn guarding the Lötschental, and the great icy highway of the Grosser Aletschgletscher. Plus, of course, numerous others wait to surprise anyone with an inquisitive nature and an eye to see beyond mountains of celebrity.

The Central Swiss Alps

There are few mountains of celebrity among the Central Swiss Alps – those mountain groups north-east of the Oberland – but there's no shortage of scenes to gladden the eye, together with enough valleys to explore to last a dozen Alpine summers. If there is such a thing as mountain celebrity here, it'll be found on the Rigi, whose funicular-gained crown looks out across the Lake of Luzern to a distant parade of snow-peaks. Rigi has been attracting visitors since the dawn of Alpine tourism. Indeed, it was the fame of this summit view that caused Victor Hugo to comment: 'In the face of this indescribable spectacle, one understands why the half-wits swarm throughout Switzerland and Savoy.'

Yet there are many more viewpoints that are unsung and unvisited by Hugo's 'half-wits', despite their impressive beauty; viewpoints discovered only by those prepared to wander the valleys and trails of the heartland. Some of the best are found in canton Uri, whose highest peaks form the so-called Urner Oberland in an arc of glacial mountains that rim the Göschenertal.

Without question the Göschenertal is one of the most beautiful and rewarding valleys of the Central Swiss Alps. A barricade of high peaks generously plastered with ice and snow blocks its western end and sends out long ridge systems to enclose tributary glens in a wild embrace. Several huts have been built in spectacular locations, linked by paths that weave among tiny pools, boggy corners and overflowing cushions of alpenrose. As with the greater part of the Alpine chain, the majority of peaks here are known only to the local enthusiast or the connoisseur whose field of vision ranges beyond the known and familiar. Yet their elegance of form and stature offer no poor second best to the lover of wild places.

The Göschenertal drains into the Reuss, which flows north to the Urnersee. A little short of the lake Altdorf lies at the foot of the Schächental, a valley that climbs eastward to the Klausenpass. From that road, between Unterschächen and the pass itself, a view is gained of a spectacular waterfall that bursts from the southern mountain flank in a great rush of spray above the tiny hamlet of Äsch. A path descends from the pass to that hamlet, while other trails climb above the cascade in an exploration of yet more secretive country rich in vegetation and big mountain views. One of those trails descends abruptly into the lovely Brunnital, which flows out to Unterschächen.

Again, this little-known valley would stand comparison with the finest in all the Swiss Alps. Aligned south to north, it's a seductive, steep-sided glen that drains a fabulous amphitheatre which rises in a 1600 metre wall above the last alp hamlet. Among the high peaks here, the best are undoubtedly the Gross Ruchen and Gross Windgällen.

There are two sets of Windgällen peaks located either side of the Schachental. Those of the north flank can be reached by way of the charming Bisistal; while those of the south overlook the Maderanertal, which flows from an outlier of the 3614 metre Tödi. Known as the 'King of Little Mountains', the Tödi commands the upper Linthal in the Glarner Alps, which fall away to the Walensee, that fjord-like lake whose steep north bank rises to the breaking-wave ridge of the Churfirsten, seen by all who travel the autobahn from Zürich to Chur. And from that ridge eyes are drawn north again to the limestone block of the Alpstein, crowned by the Säntis – a mountain grossly disfigured by hideous constructions, yet whose ridges, consort peaks and surrounding valleys offer sublime scenes and adventure for all.

The Rätikon and Silvretta Alps

Carrying the Austro-Swiss border above the valleys of Prättigau and Lower Engadine to the south, and Montafon in the Vorarlberg to the north, the fairly small but immensely attractive groups of the Rätikon and Silvretta Alps define the outer limits of this collection of Central Alps. The first rewards with utterly delightful hut-to-hut tours; the second offers first-season ascents in a truly Alpine setting of glacier and snowfield among mountains that seem much bigger than they really are. Despite being close neighbours that continue a common boundary line, the two groups are visually and geologically very different from one another, yet their scenic qualities are equally fine. Lush green meadows lie below the Rätikon's limestone frontier wall, but between meadow and rockface a chaos of scree and boulder creates a no-man's land filled in early summer with a wealth of flowering plants.

The crystalline Silvretta range mimics the scenery of the Bernese or Pennine Alps – but on a smaller, more intimate scale, with glaciers spilling from high fields of névé on the Austrian side, and mostly snow-free slopes above Swiss valleys. Its highest summit, Piz Linard (3411m), is almost entirely rock, standing away from the frontier ridge as a pyramid soaring above the Engadine's pronounced 'S' bend.

Among the Rätikon only its highest peak, the Schesaplana, hangs onto a final segment of glacier in its upper reaches, while elsewhere exotic rock fingers and turrets imitate the Dolomites of South Tyrol, balancing all the while tilted blocks of karst in place of snowfields and glaciers.

The two sides of the Silvretta Alps could hardly be more different. Deep valleys squeeze up their southern, mostly snow-free slopes. Most of these coming in from the Lower Engadine are fairly short, but from Klosters in the Prättigau region a long finger of valley prods eastward between extensive ridge systems before coming up against those mountains that form the frontier crest. Here the Silvrettahorn spills its ice above the Silvretta hut, while a side glen, rising above the Sardasca alp, takes strong walkers on a tough day's hike over the mountains to the Tübinger hut on the Austrian flank. On the northern side, glaciers still clothe most of the Silvretta's highest peaks – Piz Buin and the Dreiländerspitze being typical examples – and set the theme to be continued by the long, crystalline range that extends eastward along Austria's southern borders.

Moving from one group to the next across interlinking ridges is to experience the diverse nature of the Alps in miniature, providing yet another reason to celebrate their infinite variety.

* * *

Pass to Pass across the Swiss Alps

The seventh morning of our trek across the Central Alps dawned grey and forbidding. A cold drizzle leaked from clouds that settled on rooftops as we set out for our next pass. Not once that day did the clouds lift, nor even did they give a hint that in them were mountains of three and four thousand metres; huge slabs of limestone, snowfields, glaciers and icefalls.

On gaining our pass, instead of descending into the valley on the other side to the warm welcome that villages extend on such days, we remained high and strayed to the right along a barely visible trail across damp pasture with the sound of cowbells ringing far off. An hour and a half later we stumbled into the building for which we'd been aiming, and spent the night in a small dormitory lost among the clouds.

Morning brought a revelation. Before dawn we were outside, marooned above a cloud-sea waiting for the sunrise whose first arrows glanced across giants of the Bernese Oberland. Above the mountains the sky was clear, but below two thousand metres the world had been drowned. Stranded on our island of grass, we were uplifted by the glories of the new day that burst upon us in a globe of fire from the east. Another gift had been won.

The Alpine Pass Route makes a multi-day traverse of Switzerland from Sargans near the Walensee in the east to Montreux on the Lake of Geneva more than 300 kilometres and 16 passes later. Exploring the Glarner, Uri, Bernese and Vaudoise Alps, the route unveils a wide range of mountain grandeur over a fortnight or so of wandering, and is rightly considered to be one of the most rewarding of Alpine treks.

Not only does this route nudge close to many of the best-known peaks, it also gives an opportunity to view them from a respectable distance in order to appreciate their proper scale. And it also introduces numerous 'unknown' mountain groups and barely-visited alps, as well as valleys and villages virtually untouched by the tourist trade. It exposes a workaday side of the range and, over successive days, teaches the best of all geography lessons as you work your way over one ridge after another.

However, perhaps the most important lesson taught by the APR is that the Alps are not yet overcrowded or sacrificed for tourist gold. Especially in the early days of the trek one may walk for many hours without seeing another human being, be they trekker, climber or farmer. The contrast between days in the Glarner and Uri Alps, and the trek's central section from Engelberg to Kandersteg, is extreme, while the scenic variety is at all times enriching.

Lac de Fenêtre

Pennine Alps

The Swiss Val Ferret acts as a buffer zone between the eastern limits of the Mont Blanc range and the start of the Pennine Alps. It's a gentle, green valley, distinctly pastoral in nature and with little in the way of tourist infrastructure. Farming communities nestle among meadows that are pocked with lichen-stained granaries and barns, and large herds of cattle graze the upper pastures. Tucked under the Swiss-Italian border at its head, the Lacs de Fenêtre are shallow tarns with marshy banks fluffed with cotton grass. Looking west across the unseen valley to outliers of the Mont Blanc range, the mountain at the extreme left of the picture is the Grandes Jorasses. Then come the Aiguilles de Leschaux, Talèfre and Triolet, with the splendid Mont Dolent at the far end of the ridge carrying a long strip of glacier. It is on Mont Dolent's summit that the borders of France, Switzerland and Italy all converge, while the prominent peak above the right-hand glacier is the Tour Noir.

Storm clouds over Lac de Fenêtre

Pennine Alps

Creating a multi-day circuit of the Combin massif late one summer, a friend and I came over the mountains from Italy into Switzerland west of the Col du Grand St Bernard by way of the rocky Fenêtre de Ferret, and there discovered the idyllic Lacs de Fenêtre gleaming on their grassy shelf high above the Val Ferret. Attracted by their apparently remote situation, by the flowers, rocks and streams, and by the utterly magical views which were too good to ignore, we spent the afternoon lazing on their banks in order to absorb the unique perfection of the scene. For some time the day matched in almost every respect the winter dreams that had inspired our summer's campaign. But we failed to take note of the changing light conditions and ignored ominous signs of a deterioration, and an hour after the previous photograph was taken a storm swept across the Mont Blanc range and exploded about us. Summer turned to winter and snow fell for the next two days.

Silhouettes outside Cabane du Mont Fort

Pennine Alps

The downhill ski industry has had a profound effect on the right-hand slopes of Val de Bagnes above Le Châble. With Verbier at its hub, a veritable lacework of cables has destroyed any semblance of wilderness. And yet, where mechanical intrusion ends a choice of trails cuts east and south-east across the mountains, teasing well away from ski tows and cable-cars and offering some extraordinary views. Perched at 2457 metres, Cabane du Mont Fort makes a near-perfect base from which to explore some of these trails. It is early evening, and a group of trekkers sits outside the hut and watches as, moment by moment, the light changes. This is an especially relaxing time – the day's efforts are over, a meal and a bed for the night are assured, and there are no immediate demands that will disturb this opportunity to absorb the hut's location and atmosphere. Later, the trekkers will no doubt reflect on the day just gone and plan tomorrow's route. But for now it is enough simply to sit – and enjoy the moment.

Mont Blanc floats on a raft of mist

Pennine Alps

Minutes after the previous image was taken, the setting sun had started to cast its low, near-horizontal beams across the Alps, spilling colours that have no time to settle before they're absorbed and transformed by the changing atmosphere. On the horizon, three days' trek away, the Mont Blanc range floats on a raft of mist that grows more dense as night arrives to fill the hidden valleys. It is then that we who are staying at the hut find ourselves marooned above the clouds in a magical realm that hovers somewhere (in Rébuffet's words) between heaven and earth. Every few moments someone will grab a camera and wander outside in an attempt to capture the ever-changing light conditions; couples and small groups stand transfixed, lost in their own thoughts, soaking the peace as the timeless drama of sunset is played out around them. In life there are moments as big as years. This is one of them, and we are anxious not to lose it.

Mont Blanc de Cheilon

Pennine Alps

Two crossing points, only a few metres apart, cut into the long transverse ridge that pushes north from Pigne d'Arolla to form a divide between Val des Dix and the Val d'Arolla stem of Val d'Hérens. The first of these is Col de Riedmatten, a steep, gritty couloir leading to a narrow cleft at 2919 metres; while the other is the slightly lower Pas de Chèvres, easy on its east side, but walled on the west by steep crags surmounted by three near-vertical ladders. Both crossing places offer a very different experience from the other, and different views too. Thanks to its abrupt side walls, Col de Riedmatten blinkers the walker or climber who arrives there, but as you emerge through to the Arolla side and descend a short way, a surprise view shows the triangular north face of Mont Blanc de Cheilon across the dip of Pas de Chèvres. Although it is on show throughout the trek through Val des Dix, framed as it is here by the shadowed foreground ridge, this is my preferred view of the mountain.

Eastward view from Pas de Chèvres

Pennine Alps

Arriving at the top of the Pas de Chèvres ladders walkers are rewarded by a foreground scene of jumbled rock and scree, of moraine highway and debris-covered glacier – a genesis land upon which nature has yet to set patterns of vegetation. Or so it seems. In many respects this is a drab, almost monochrome landscape. Yet one sees beyond that initial impression, for a complex middle ground of peak and ridge gives a promise of greater things to come. As you descend towards Arolla beyond this seemingly barren land, then turn a spur and are suddenly drawn across lush slopes of pasture and pinewood, that promise is fulfilled. Cushions of saxifrage add colour to the moraine bank, and marmots penetrate the silence with their warning whistle. Such are the contrasts and pleasures of the Walker's Haute Route which leads across the grain of the Pennine Alps from Chamonix to Zermatt. Each pass crossed presents a new landscape to be unravelled; each stage rewards with a multitude of experience.

Moiry glacier and Pointes de Mourti

Pennine Alps

Seen from the right-hand lateral moraine of the Moiry glacier, the Pointes de Mourti are divided by a smooth-looking ramp of a hanging glacier suspended over an ice-filled basin. Ice dominates this upper valley, and the route to the Cabane de Moiry – whose roof can be seen on the rock spur at the far left of this photograph – follows the crest of moraine overlooking the glacier before descending briefly into its ablation trough, from which the way then rises in steep zigzags to the hut. The Moiry glacier is often used by mountain guides and climbing school leaders to teach techniques of crevasse rescue, but like so many Alpine icefields today, it is receding at an alarming rate, as any frequent visitor will affirm. However, it remains an impressive landscape feature, and trekkers following the Walker's Haute Route from Chamonix to Zermatt are encouraged to make this diversion to the hut in order to experience not only the glacial world, but the 'big mountain' atmosphere of a night spent at the *cabane*.

Icefall of the Moiry glacier

Pennine Alps

Few huts accessible to walkers give a closer prospect of an icefall than that of Cabane de Moiry. Owned by the Montreux Section of the SAC, and built on a rocky promontory at 2825 metres below the Aiguilles de la Lé, it provides a clear and unobstructed view of what the pioneer A.W. Moore described as a 'great cascade of séracs'. Visitors to the hut study this cascade from a safe vantage point, and watch as lofty blue or grey towers occasionally collapse with an explosive roar and fill the air with ice crystals. Moore was deeply impressed, not only by the icefall but by the Moiry glacier as a whole, calling it 'a noble ice-stream, comparable to any other in the Alps' (*The Alps in 1864*). The icefall is contained between rock walls, but below it the glacier smooths into a long stream riven with crevasses and flanked by perfectly formed moraine banks. From the hut terrace one looks down onto a perfect example of an Alpine glacier and, beyond its snout, to the valley it carved long ago.

Sunset clouds, Cabane de Moiry

Pennine Alps

Another mountain day draws to a close as shadows hasten through the valley, sweep up the glacier and enclose Cabane de Moiry in their embrace. Far beyond the mountains the dying sun leaves scorched clouds in its wake, and turns the ridge on the west side of the Moiry glacier into a blackened profile whose individual features will remain obscured until tomorrow's daybreak. The low point of that ridge is Col de la Couronne (2987m) which, despite offering the most direct route between La Forclaz and the Moiry hut, is rarely used on account of rockfall danger in a couloir on its western side. Rising from the col to the right is the 3101 metre Clocher de Couronne at the start of the south-east ridge of Couronne de Bréona. According to the Alpine Club guidebook, the Couronne has some of the finest rock hereabouts, in direct contrast to that of the high point on the left, Pointe de Moiry (3303m), whose poor reputation deters most climbers looking for sport in the neighbourhood.

Tsijière de la Vatse and the Moming glacier

Pennine Alps

Val d'Anniviers must count as the grandest of all valleys in the Pennine Alps –
a long, deep trench that seduces towards its head with stunning high mountain
scenery. Zinal is its highest village; beyond it lies an icebound cirque, with
another cutting back to the left. One of the finest and steepest walks here
crosses the high point of Roc de la Vache on a spur jutting from Point d'Ar
Pitetta south-east of Zinal. Two hundred metres below the Roc stands the
abandoned alp hut of Tsijière de la Vatse – its old stone walls crumbling, its
shingle roof warped and leaking. From the hut, though, the full majesty of the
Ar Pitetta cirque's south wall is suddenly revealed in all its ice-clad splendour.
Here we see the sparkling mass of the Moming glacier tumbling from a pristine
snow pelmet slung between the dark rock peak of Lo Besso and Pointe Sud de
Moming. As you descend below the hut, the cirque opens to the left, where its
lofty headwall culminates in the Weisshorn, one of the truly great Alpine peaks.

Cabane d'Ar Pitetta

Pennine Alps

Approached by a walk of four hours or so from Zinal, the small, stone-built Cabane d'Ar Pitetta is located high in the Ar Pitetta cirque among moraines spilling down from the Weisshorn's glacier. At 2786 metres, and with dormitory places for 30, it's a romantically wild setting for a hut whose outlook is dominated by towering rock and cascades of ice. Yet this view of the cirque's south wall is severely foreshortened and confused by a wilderness of moraine, rock rib and icefall. Seen here following a late summer fall of snow, one can appreciate the hut's snug security, for when Whymper and Moore came to the cirque in July 1864 prior to making the first crossing of the Moming pass, they were forced to spend a night in an alp chalet some way below the present *cabane*. According to Whymper: 'It was a hovel, growing, as it were, out of the hill-side; roofed with rough slabs of slaty stone; without a door or window; surrounded by quagmires of ordure, and dirt of every description' (*Scrambles Amongst the Alps*).

Ober Gabelhorn and the Zinal glacier

Pennine Alps

Blocking the head of Val de Zinal – the upper reaches of Val d'Anniviers – the graceful Ober Gabelhorn (4063m) commands a major ridge system whose south side falls to the Zmutt valley above Zermatt. Seen here from the north-west, this most elegant of mountains overlooks a confluence of glaciers – the Durand, spilling from the Gabelhorn itself, joins forces with the Cornier on the right to become the Glacier de Zinal, seen pushing downvalley below the walkers. The moraine path in the foreground was for many years taken by the route to the Cabane du Mountet, crossing the glacier a short distance beyond where this photograph was taken. But with the moraine crest breaking up in several places, and glacial recession making the crossing a less attractive proposition, an alternative path was created on the opposite side of the valley. That path makes a traverse of the steep flank of Lo Besso and is a remarkable piece of engineering, but it is less visually inspiring than this one, despite some huge mountains in view.

Grand Cornier and Dent Blanche

Pennine Alps

Falling just a few metres short of the magical 4000 metre mark, the Grand Cornier – seen here appearing to overshadow its loftier neighbour, the Dent Blanche – is nonetheless an impressive mountain, whose north-east face holds a major ice route first climbed in 1932. Though it may be difficult to believe from this viewpoint on the path to Cabane du Mountet south of Zinal, the face has lost a lot of its ice over recent years, and stonefall is a major hazard for climbers attempting it. Walkers, on the other hand, making their way to the Mountet hut, are able to study the face from a safe distance across the valley. It's just one of several uplifting views to be harvested from this path, although what is missing until almost the last moment is sight of the valley's headwall dominated by the Ober Gabelhorn – as indicated by the previous photograph. In truth, every path in the upper Val d'Anniviers will reward with scenes of dramatic beauty, for it's one of the finest of all Alpine valleys.

Bishorn and Weisshorn from the Turtmanntal

Pennine Alps

Wedged between Val d'Anniviers and the Mattertal that leads to Zermatt, the Turtmanntal has a delightfully remote 'lost world' ambience. Apart from a single hotel, an inn and a Swiss Alpine Club hut, the valley has little in the way of tourist infrastructure, and the little village of Gruben is deserted in winter. The Victorian pioneer Leslie Stephen celebrated its remoteness in *The Playground of Europe*, and much of his description of the valley remains true today. Of several crossings into the Turtmanntal from the Val d'Anniviers, by far the best is via the 2874 metre Forcletta – itself a splendid vantage point. As you descend from it into the valley, you come to the alp of Chalte Berg on a shelf of rough pasture to gain this view of the Bishorn, flanked by the Bruneg (left) and Turtmann glaciers, and with the Weisshorn seen to the right of the Bishorn's summit – 'one of the most sublime aspects of that almost faultless mountain' is how Stephen described it.

Nadelhorn, Dom and the Ried glacier

Pennine Alps

When trekking from Chamonix to Zermatt over projecting ridges of the Pennine Alps, the final crossing is by way of the wind-scoured Augstbordpass, which leads from the Turtmanntal to the Mattertal. After descending into a rocky basin where the maniacal cry of the capercaillie is sometimes to be heard, the path forks. Edging right, the way soon turns a spur and comes to this vantage point – one of the grandest of the whole route. St Niklaus lies some 1200 metres below, but across the valley the long trunk of the Ried glacier sweeps down from the Nadelhorn, while the 4545 metre summit of the Dom – highest mountain entirely in Switzerland – can be detected at the crowning point of the right-hand glacier. Meanwhile the trekker is gazing towards the head of the valley where, 30 kilometres away, a massive wall of snow and ice carries the Italian border above Zermatt. From here all the way down to St Niklaus that vision acts as a constant lure.

Jungen, above St Niklaus

Pennine Alps

Huddled together as if for mutual protection on the lip of a precariously steep slope, almost 900 metres above the Mattervispa river, the group of typical Valaisian haybarns (*mazots*), chalets, restaurant and tiny white-walled chapel make Jungen one of the most attractive and dramatically situated hamlets in all Switzerland. It is September, and farmers rake the final hay crop before the autumn rains settle in and everyone moves down to the valley. A small do-it-yourself cable-car links the hamlet with St Niklaus, but to my mind it's far better to approach Jungen from above – from the Jungtal hanging valley, perhaps, or from Moosalp along a waymarked *höhenweg* or, better still, after crossing the Augstbordpass – for then the true drama of its location, and the sheer grandeur of its views, can be fully appreciated. Across the depths of the hinted at, but unseen Mattertal the chalets of Gasenried, neighbour to Grächen, can be seen in this photograph. That, too, is a charming village at the start of the Europaweg which leads walkers to Zermatt.

Mist wreaths over the Mattertal

Pennine Alps

The magic of early autumn comes to the Mattertal. Trees have yet to attract the Midas touch of October, but mist wreaths hang over the valley until the sun's warmth manages to penetrate this steep-walled cleft. Having spent the night in Jungen, I woke to see the Breithorn closing off the head of the valley with a dazzle of sun on snow, but shadows remain in the Mattertal from Täsch down. Only we here in Jungen, and the few huts of Sparru and Teli set upon their meagre terraces on the western slope, gather the light. The Swiss-Italian frontier ridge in the distance extends left of the Breithorn over Pollux and Castor, while to its right, and dwarfed by the great bulk of the Breithorn itself, is the Klein Matterhorn – the Matterhorn proper is hidden from view by a succession of intervening shoulders and spurs. Recently a trail has been created along this right-hand wall, matching a section of the Europaweg which runs along the left-hand slope. Both are challenging but rewarding routes.

The Matterhorn from Höhbalmen

Pennine Alps

One of the most satisfying of all outings from Zermatt climbs through the Trift gorge then crosses the high pastureland of Höhbalmen, a wonderful grassy belvedere from which to study many of the 4000 metre peaks that rim the huge catchment area of the upper Mattertal. The Matterhorn naturally focuses much of one's attention here. Rising across the deep Zmutt valley, the precipitous north face – in shadow – is flanked on the left by the Hörnli ridge, and on the right by the Zmutt. Generally considered one of the six major north faces of the Alps, it was first climbed by the brothers Schmid from Münich in 1931. That is just one background feature, though, to walks that abound here. The main path forks – with one route descending directly to Zermatt, while the other crosses the saddle in this photograph, then makes a traverse high above the Zmutt valley before dropping to it through the Arben glen. And every step of the way is a celebration of high mountain scenery.

Dent d'Hérens from the Schönbiel hut

Pennine Alps

Standing on the lateral moraine of the Zmutt glacier directly below the Dent Blanche, the Schönbiel hut looks across the glacier to the long east ridge and north face of the Dent d'Hérens. Although this complex mountain of 4171 metres tends to be overshadowed by the illustrious Matterhorn to the east, it is nonetheless a very elegant and challenging peak, described by Geoffrey Winthrop Young as 'a lacquer of dark slab and hanging glacier, forcing the eye perpetually outward to the order of its outline' (*On High Hills*). The obvious saddle to the right of the mountain is the Tiefmattenjoch (3565m), by which the Valpelline in Italy may be reached by experienced and equipped parties, although from the Italian side the Dent d'Hérens is much less attractive or appealing than from the north. But even without the temptation of such a crossing, or of the prospect of climbing the mountain itself, the Schönbiel hut and its surroundings more than compensate for the four-hour approach from Zermatt.

The Schwarzsee

Pennine Alps

Nestling at the foot of the Matterhorn's Hörnli ridge, the oval-shaped Schwarzsee is probably the most visited lake in the Pennine Alps of Switzerland, thanks to its ease of access by cable-car from Zermatt. It will be a rare summer's day when its banks are not crowded with picnic parties or tourists gazing dreamily into the water. On its north shore stands the tiny chapel of Maria zum Schnee, which was built in 1780 as an offering of thanks by travellers who survived a storm nearby, while the mountain whose reflection is being cast in the water below the chapel is the Ober Gabelhorn, its great south face being the main feature on show. Between the lake and the Ober Gabelhorn lies the Zmutt valley, and a delightful series of trails descend into it, providing on the way abrupt but foreshortened views of the Matterhorn's north face. On the descent through the valley a path visits both Stafelalp and Zmutt, finally entering Zermatt in about three hours. This makes a very fine walk with memorable views throughout.

Ober Gabelhorn from the slopes of the Matterhorn

Pennine Alps

The steep trail that leads from the Schwarzsee up to the Hörnli hut on the Matterhorn is highly recommended for the richness of its panoramic views. As you gain height the surrounding landscape is slowly unravelled, valleys fall away and you begin to see across ridges that had previously marked the limit of your horizon to a maze of peaks, glaciers and high snowfields whose apparent complexity gradually recedes. In place of confusion comes a semblance of order as the geography of the region begins to make sense. Many of the features seen here are visible from other paths reaching out from Zermatt, but the Hörnli trail provides a unique perspective, as this photograph shows. On the left is the Ober Gabelhorn, its impressive south face rising for 600 metres above the snow ramp at its foot. Then comes the snow crest of the Wellenkuppe, with the remarkable stiletto point a little right of centre being the Zinal Rothorn. The famed Weisshorn appears to the right of that, like a vast triangular wall of rock.

View from the Hörnli hut terrace

Pennine Alps

The terrace outside the Hörnli hut and adjacent Berghotel Matterhorn (formerly known as the Belvedere Hotel) makes a stunning viewpoint from which to study the majestic wall of 4000 metre snowpeaks whose summits carry the Swiss-Italian frontier. Although it is quite naturally the Matterhorn which draws everyone here, from the ordinary walker to ambitious climber, it has to be said that a close view of that rocky pyramid can be somewhat disappointing. It is, in fact, a disintegrating monolith without the grace of form one normally imagines. But the eastward view is very different and much more enticing. The north flank of the Breithorn is on the right of the picture, with the great bulk of Monte Rosa marking the birth of the Gornerglacier at the left-hand end of the wall. The panorama of course extends far beyond the limits imposed by the camera lens, and includes a ticker's list of great Alpine peaks. If for no other reason than to enjoy such a panorama, the 677 metre climb from the Schwarzsee is worth tackling.

The Mischabel wall from Plattjen

Pennine Alps

The Plattjen gondola lift gives access to a lofty shoulder above Saas Fee. From here one gains not only an amazing aerial view of the Saastal stretching off to the north but a view west, too, across the Saas basin to the great Mischabel wall, whose summits include the Täschhorn, Dom, Lenzspitze and Nadelhorn. It is this immense wall of 4000 metre peaks that forms the most spectacular section of a glacial cirque within which Saas Fee is contained. Below the glaciers a path known as the Gemsweg sweeps round from Plattjen to Hannig – in effect from one side of the cirque to the other – to create a three-hour walk of great beauty. Another path which also begins at the upper station of the Plattjen lift edges south along an exposed, and what seems near-vertical, slope of the Mittaghorn and Egginer, high above the toy-like buildings of Saas Almagell, as an approach route to the Britannia hut. Both paths give rewarding walks noted for their extensive vistas.

Strahlhorn, Rimpfischhorn and the Allalin glacier

Pennine Alps

Supported by financial donations from the ABMSAC (Association of British Members of the Swiss Alpine Club), the large and well-appointed Britannia hut stands in a small cleft below the Klein Allalin, between the Chessjen and Hohlaub glaciers. Reached in no more than about 40 minutes from the Felskinn lift on a marked route over the Egginerjoch and along a near-level glacier, or in two hours from the Plattjen gondola, the hut was extended in 1997 and is regularly used as a base for ascents of such peaks as the Strahlhorn, Rimpfischhorn, Allalinhorn and Alphubel, as well as classic glacier crossings such as that of the Adler pass to reach Zermatt. A short walk from the hut leads onto the Klein Allalin at 3069 metres, from where this image was taken. It shows the Strahlhorn on the left and the rocky Rimpfischhorn rising from the Allalin glacier. The Adler pass is the snow saddle between the two peaks, and the Hohlaub glacier is the icefield at bottom right.

Gspon and the Bietschhorn

Pennine Alps

Reached by a two-stage cable-car from Stalden at the confluence of the Saastal and Mattertal, the chalets of Gspon are scattered across a neatly shaved hillside at the northern end of the Saas valley. It's a tranquil, traffic-free little village open to the sun and facing west. Beyond it to the north lies the Rhône valley, on the far side of which rises the graceful point of the Bietschhorn. With this sublime outlook Gspon is a restful place to spend a few days, but it also marks the starting point for one of the great walks of the Saastal, the so-called Gspon Höhenweg. This splendid route ripples along the east slope of the valley for 13 kilometres, ending in Saas Grund, but offers an alternative high finish where the Kreuzboden gondola lift suggests an easy way down to the valley. Even better is to link this walk with the Höhenweg Almagelleralp for a further 10 kilometres, but only really fit walkers should attempt this in one day.

Val d'Osura

Lepontine Alps

Deep within the heart of the Alps of canton Ticino on the south side of the Alpine watershed Val Verzasca, whose lower reaches spill into Lago Maggiore, is fed by a number of tributary glens, most of which are uninhabited. At Brione the valley forks. The north-west branch is the charming Val d'Osura, a real gem of a valley with a few rustic houses and their barns slumbering in scant pastureland. This track pushes deeper into the valley, and when it gives way a path climbs into the Sambuco cirque under Monte Zucchero. After brushing among wild raspberry canes, alpenrose and rowan thickets, the path comes to the unmanned Capanna Alpe d'Osola, which has room for about a dozen in a hauntingly unfussed setting. There may be no great peaks here, no glaciers or permanent fields of snow, but wherever you wander in the Osura glen your experience will be something akin to that of the Victorian pioneers when they explored the Alps more than a hundred years ago. And there's immense satisfaction in that.

Lepontine stream and water-worn slabs

Lepontine Alps

Crystal streams drain the inner valleys of the Lepontine Alps. Up here in the untamed recesses of these mountains there are no polluting industries, no agricultural waste products to poison the land and discolour the rivers, and few villages or farmhouses either. So streams that are born high up where the last glacial remnants shrivel in the hot Lombardy-brushed summers are filtered through screes, mossy beds and coarse meadows. Cascades spill over granite slabs into pools that lie calm and seductively cool among the sun-warmed rocks and boulders, where you can stretch out for hours and watch as unsuspecting trout flick their tails in the shallows and butterflies settle on your bare arms. Some of these river beds have been scoured into patterned whorls, with bleached ribs and moulded grooves that display strips of grey, black or (when wet) blue, like the grain of well-seasoned timber. Among them idle rivers slip gently from one level to the next until, that is, a sudden summer storm comes to change their mood.

Haymaking in Valle di Peccia

Lepontine Alps

North of Valle Maggia, Val Lavizzara is one of its earliest tributaries. But this also has its own feeder valleys. Of the two upper tributaries, Valle di Peccia is the most westerly, draining as it does the southern slopes of the Cristallina massif. It's a pleasant little glen with a handful of small villages and hamlets, but in common with many districts within the Lepontine Alps there has been a decline in farming over the past 50 years, and a number of its high alps are now deserted and overgrown, as are some of its footpaths. Yet still a few hardy families continue to work the land, gathering three or more hay crops each summer to feed their cattle when winter snow denies access to the meadows. It's a lonely existence in these high alps and one wonders how much longer this method of farming will continue. In some valleys old farmhouses have been given a new lease of life as holiday homes, but many buildings crumble into the pastures to be smothered by vegetation or adopted by sun-loving lizards.

Lago di Sambuco

Lepontine Alps

High above Val Lavizzara a steep trail descends nearly 800 metres from Lago di Mognola to the pastel-shaded village of Fusio, the valley's highest community. Beyond Fusio in the upper valley, which bites into the Cristallina massif, a dam holds back the waters of Lago di Sambuco, one of a series of lakes in the granitelands of the Cristallina mountains to have been harnessed to generate electricity. Down there the hydro-engineers have left a few scars, but where we had been on the day this photograph was taken was prime walking country. It is an abrupt landscape with little out of place – an alp or two, one of which had goats sleeping on the roof of a chalet; a few cascades from unguessed heights; and a tarn trapped in a bowl of mountains at over 2000 metres. There was a grassy saddle with eye-watering views and, apart from our laboured breathing, only the sounds of nature at rest. In fact, just the setting for another perfect Alpine day.

Val Roseg headwall

Bernina Alps

Named after Dr Johann Coaz, the man who made the first ascent of Piz Bernina, the Coaz hut stands at the far end of Val Roseg overlooking its glacial headwall. One of the most scenic ways to approach this hut entails crossing the 2755 metre Fuorcla Surlej and taking a high path across the slopes of Piz Corvatsch. It was from this path that the photograph was taken on a crisp September morning at the tail-end of the season. Dazzled by the brilliance of sun on ice, I sat perched upon a rock to study the antics of a pair of marmots as they made preparations for their six-month hibernation, and rejoiced in the valley's gift of peace. Apart from the marmots I had the world to myself. At the head of the valley, just left of centre, the ear-like formations are those of the twin Sella peaks (3584m and 3564m), while the rocky fin to the right of them is Piz Glüschaint at 3594 metres. The Coaz hut stands below Piz Glüschaint among shining rocks above the obvious moraine rib.

Alpe Fora and Monte Disgrazia

Bregaglia Alps

Considerably higher than any of its neighbours in the Bregaglia Alps, the isolated Monte Disgrazia, with its noble outline and classic proportions, has the reputation of being one of the most beautiful mountains in the Alps. Seen here from the old stone huts of Alpe Fora on the south side of the Bernina Group, we see its great north flank across the depths of Val Malenco. This is a tremendous viewpoint and a site worth visiting for itself, and there's another nearby on the way to Rifugio Longoni where a small tarn makes a gleaming foreground while waterfalls spill down crags behind. But there are many other fine vantage points, too, that similarly display Disgrazia's undisputed charms. One such is to be found on the descent from the Muretto pass, where a more direct northerly aspect is on show, while yet another reveals its south-west face from the delightful meadows of Valle Preda Rossa. In fact from almost any angle Monte Disgrazia has the ability to both please and impress.

The Silsersee and Piz Corvatsch

Upper Engadine

Neighbouring the Bernina Alps, the Engadine valley gives rise to the River Inn. In its upper reaches between Maloja and St Moritz, the valley sparkles with a string of lakes lying at an altitude of around 1800 metres. This is a district that will always repay the attention of walkers, for with delightful tributary glens such as the Vals Fex and Fedoz, and balcony trails that trace hillsides on both sides of the valley, there's plenty to choose from. On the left flank a number of trails have been linked together to create the Via Engiadina, a route stretching the length of both the Upper and Lower Engadine. In its early stages near the few houses of Blaunca, a brief diversion from that trail rewards with an uninterrupted view overlooking the Silsersee, with the little hamlet of Isola on the spit of land projecting into the lake at the foot of Piz Corvatsch. In winter, when the lakes are frozen over, the Engadine cross-country ski marathon takes place here, with thousands of skiers racing across the icy surface.

Piz Cristanas, Val Sesvenna

Lower Engadine

Mountains on the north side of the Lower Engadine form part of the Silvretta Alps, a range shared with Austria. But those on the south side of the valley, reaching up to the Italian border but not included within the Swiss National Park's boundaries, belong to a group that enjoys very little publicity outside Switzerland. It is, however, a region rich in wildlife and full of charm that would repay a number of visits. Working your way south out of Scuol into an undeveloped glen, pass below the so-called Engiadina Dolomites and you'll eventually come to the neat little hamlet of S-charl, where a fine choice of walking routes set out to explore the valley's upper tributaries. The closest is Val Sesvenna, seen here with Piz Cristanas still wearing the last of winter's snow. Curving right at the foot of that peak, a trail climbs over Fuorcla Sesvenna into the Italian Valle di Slingia as part of an agreeable circular tour. But this is just one of several walking routes possible from a base in S-charl.

The Eiger, seen from Grosse Scheidegg

Bernese Alps

The usual route of approach to Grindelwald is from Interlaken and along the valley of the Schwarze Lütschine. But walkers coming from the east, along the Alpine Pass Route, for example, reach the Grosse Scheidegg to discover a surprise view onto an open, chalet-freckled basin, with a massive wall of peaks stretching ahead. Left of centre the first peak is the Mattenberg, whose ridge runs out of the frame to the Schreckhorn. The snow summit is that of the Mönch, and the sharp rock peak is the Eiger, whose north face casts a shadow onto the distant Kleine Scheidegg. The sunlit triangular rockface in the centre of the picture guards the entrance to a remarkable glacial amphitheatre, while the deep, shadow-edged 'V' below the Mattenberg indicates the location of the Upper Grindelwald glacier's gorge. The narrow path in the foreground is part of the Höhenweg 2400, which angles across sloping pastureland on the way to First with more breathtaking views to enjoy all the way. One glance from Grosse Scheidegg, then, is sufficient to underscore Grindelwald's great walking potential.

Tackling the Rots Gufer below the Schreckhorn hut

Bernese Alps

The effects of glacial recession and crumbling moraines add a frisson of excitement to a visit to the Schreckhorn hut in the heart of the Bernese Alps. After passing through the rocky gorge carved by the Lower Grindelwald glacier and entering the vast ice-carved cirque dominated by the Fiescherwand, the trail passes the small Stieregg restaurant, picks a way over moraine debris and climbs to a surprise patch of grassland with a view of the icefall of the Obers Eismeer glacier directly ahead. Frozen turrets, towers and digits of blue ice lean at crazy angles before toppling with a shudder and a roar onto the lower reaches of the glacier, while the continuing route to the hut edges close to this icefall and ascends the rock band of the Rots Gufer by a series of fixed cables and other aids. The family seen here descending to the Rots Gufer have taken the sensible precaution of safeguarding the children with a length of rope.

Finsteraarhorn and Fiescherwand

Bernese Alps

Coming out of the vast pastureland of Bussalp above Grindelwald, a group of walkers enjoys one of the great panoramic views of the Oberland. From the lower pastures only a vague hint may be deduced of splendours to come, but as the trail rises and draws close to the crest of this spur, so the mountains burst into view. The elegant sharp-tipped peak on the far left of the scene is the Finsteraarhorn, at 4274 metres the highest of the Bernese Alps, while the immense cornice-topped rockface at centre right is that of the Fiescherwand. Walled by the Fiescherwand, a great ice-scoured amphitheatre is barely perceived from Grindelwald, which lies near its entrance 1000 metres or so below the grass crest of the foreground. With only a little effort, this and many more amazing scenes are within reach. The resort is, of course, understandably popular year-round, and although there are numerous honeypot sites and certain trails that are constantly busy it's not difficult to find solitude amid some of the most spectacular mountain scenery of all.

The Gspaltenhorn above Mürren

Bernese Alps

Though enjoying a mostly open site facing south and east, Mürren is sheltered by projecting ridges and ridge-spurs that protect it from the north and west. Some of these ridges have trails that climb onto, along and across them, and each one abounds with spectacular vantage points. One of these accessible ridges flanks the gentle Blumental, and from it you gain this view of the Gspaltenhorn, an impressive limestone peak of 3436 metres, below which lies the deep Sefinental, unseen from here. There are many impressive mountains on show from Mürren, including the Jungfrau and all those that block the head of the Lauterbrunnen valley. But although its name might not be as immediately familiar as those of many of its neighbours, the Gspaltenhorn is one of the best on account of its formidable ridges, the size of its north-east face and the great north face which soars above the Sefinental. Walkers who stray into that seemingly remote valley to visit the Rotstock hut or perhaps cross the Sefinenfurke gain a close acquaintance with this splendid mountain.

The Lauterbrunnen Breithorn

Bernese Alps

As suggested by the previous photograph, a ridge flanking the Blumental above Mürren makes a first-rate grandstand from which to study the neighbourhood and work out the geography of the district. Between the foreground ridge and that in the middle ground lies the deep Sefinental, while the mountain that captures attention is the Lauterbrunnen Breithorn, whose summit height measures 3785 metres and whose roots are firmly planted among screes, moraines and small glaciers at the end of the Lauterbrunnen valley. Forming part of the valley's headwall, it is one of at least three Swiss mountains to carry the Breithorn name: others being that on the south side of the Lötschental and the well-known Zermatt Breithorn which neighbours the Matterhorn. The rock ridge in the centre of the picture extends from the Gspaltenhorn and is crossed, just out of the frame to the left, by a steeply climbing path from the Sefinental. On the very crest lies a small meadow known as the Tanzbödeli ('the dance floor'), which is another magnificent viewpoint worth the effort to reach.

The Rottal hut

Bernese Alps

The standard approach route to the Rottal hut, located under the south-west face of the Jungfrau, is a demanding one with a steep ascent of more than 1800 metres from Stechelberg to contend with. One section uses a fixed chain as an aid to overcome an abrupt gully that splits a band of rocks; but it's well worth the effort, for at 2755 metres the hut commands a tremendous panorama. This includes not only most of the peaks that form the headwall of the Lauterbrunnen valley, but also the distant Blümlisalp massif seen in this photograph to the right of, and beyond, the right-hand snow saddle of the Tschingel pass. The hut's immediate environment is a clutter of rocks, boulders and moraine rubble, but the little hanging Rottal valley is cupped in a horseshoe of high ice-clad mountains where glaciers hang suspended from near-vertical walls. The outlook is not only inspiring both above and across the valley, but the hut is also a good place from which to study ibex.

The descent to Oberi Bundalp

Bernese Alps

Feeding into the Kandertal north-east of Kandersteg, the Kiental is a quietly unassuming valley hidden away from the Oberland tourist haunts. At the roadhead lie one or two rustic inns with dormitory accommodation at Griesalp, but above them the valley's upper reaches extend beyond alp pastures to the wild recesses of a cirque flanked by Büttlassen, Gspaltenhorn and Morgenhorn. Trekkers on the Alpine Pass Route, which makes a traverse of large sections of the Swiss Alps, come this way in order to cross the highest of the route's sixteen passes, the 2778 metre Höhturli on a shoulder of the Blümlisalp. After leaving the pastures of Oberi Bundalp, seen below, the braided trail that heads up to the pass climbs initial runnels of black scree and grit which these trekkers are beginning to descend. Although one always hopes for fine weather on the crossing of a high pass, cloud curtains add to the atmosphere and become an essential ingredient in the mountain landscape, damping the terrain, perhaps, but not our enthusiasm.

The Bietschhorn, seen from below the Lötschenpass

Bernese Alps

A crossing of the 2690 metre Lötschenpass on the high ridge dividing the Gasterntal from the Lötschental makes for an exhilarating day's trek. Located between the Balmhorn and Hockenhorn, it's the oldest glacier pass in the Bernese Alps, but the route across the glacier which hangs on the northern side is usually well marked and untroubled. As you climb from it over a series of rock terraces to gain the pass, views are severely restricted. Then suddenly you emerge to a blaze of light, and just below the privately owned hut which occupies a site by the pass this idyllic tarn is encountered. The elegant peak on the far side of the hidden Lötschental is the Bietschhorn, considered to be the most difficult to climb of all the main summits of the district. Grand though it is, the Bietschhorn is not the only mountain of note to be seen from here, for way to the south the horizon is etched by high peaks of the Pennine Alps as a snowy, serrated line.

Faldumalp in the Lötschental

Bernese Alps

Above Goppenstein on the south side of the Bernese Alps, the tiny hamlet of Faldumalp commands the length of the beautiful Lötschental as far as the icy Lötschenlücke at the head of the Langgletscher. Thanks to global warming that glacier is receding fast, but evidence of its past activity is clear to see, for it was the Langgletscher that was responsible for providing the Lötschental with its distinctive U-shape. In the summer snow and ice is in short supply in this sun-trap of a valley, but on the very crest of the Petersgrat – the ridge that runs north-east from the Lötschenpass – lies a remnant of the vast glacial sheet that during the last Ice Age covered much of the Bernese Alps. Not that any of that is evident from Faldumalp. Here it is green pasture, forest and the bare rock of the high peaks that form a backdrop, while footpaths head off in all directions to explore the slopes of this Alpine wonderland.

Weritzalp, on the Lötschentaler Höhenweg

Bernese Alps

Without question the finest walk in the Lötschental is the 15 kilometre Lötschentaler Höhenweg, which contours along the north flank of the valley at mid-height between Faldumalp and Fafleralp. Mountain and valley views are outstanding throughout, and on its way the *höhenweg* ('high path') links a string of no less than six hamlets – in addition to Faldumalp and Fafleralp, that is. Overnight accommodation is available in a few places, but most of these alps offer some form of refreshment, thereby turning the walk into what could be termed the ultimate pub-crawl. A little under halfway along the route a cableway at Lauchernalp provides a link with Wiler in the bed of the valley, but the only other option to get from one to the other is to walk. Seen here, the red-shuttered hamlet of Weritzalp is also known as Werizstafel, and is reached not long before the route begins to angle down into the valley to conclude at Fafleralp.

Gletscherstafel Wall

Bernese Alps

Descending into the Lötschental from the Petersgrat ice-cap brings you down through the steep little glen of the Uisters Tal – which also goes by the name of the Aeusseres Faflertal – in a descent of some 1300 metres over a distance of just five kilometres. It's a steep, knee-twitching descent in which you exchange gleaming ice for a more stony terrain, then precipitous slopes of grass and alpenrose; but as you lose height, so the great mass of the Glestcherstafel Wall which blocks the south side of the Lötschental appears to grow in stature ahead. At the left-hand end of the wall can be seen the Lötschentaler Breithorn, a twin-summited mountain whose highest point reaches 3785 metres, the same altitude, in fact, as its namesake at the head of the Lauterbrunnen valley. Directly ahead, at what appears to be the central point on the ridge, the shapely summit is that of the Breitlauihorn, first climbed in 1869 by the same team that made the ascent of the neighbouring Breithorn two days later.

Reflecting pool in the Göschenertal

Uri Alps

Water lies in tarns and lakes of various size right across the Alpine chain, especially where the rock is non-porous, like the solid Aare granite of the Urner Oberland east of the Bernese Alps. Near the head of the Göschenertal many tiny pools lie trapped among boulders and grey granite ledges, serving to mirror the peaks and glaciers that provide both backdrop and challenge to the visitor. In this pool it is the Dammastock Group, with its lengthy glacial apron, that receives the inverse treatment. Although there may be no 4000 metre peaks here, high mountains abound, and the valley and its Voralp tributary glen are enchanting places that reward with countless walking opportunities. Water is one of the main features of the district, not only the calm pools but in the glacial torrents, waterfalls and streams that thunder below the snowfields. Since the valley is enclosed at its western end by towering mountain walls, the only access is from the east, where Göschenen sits at the northern end of the St Gotthard tunnel below Andermatt.

Chelenalp hut

Uri Alps

The Göschenertal is one of the most beautiful valleys in the Uri Alps, walled as it is by some truly impressive ice-plastered mountains. No less than five SAC huts are accessible to walkers within the valley and its tributary, the Voralp Tal. Several of these are lodged in dress-circle seclusion, their access trails giving hours of good walking. The Chelenalp (or Kelenalp) hut is a favourite. Boldly situated at the very head of the Göschenertal within a wildly majestic cirque of high peaks, it can be reached by a walk of 3–3½ hours from the roadhead, which is served by postbus from Göschenen. Full of variety, the approach begins by crossing shrub-cushioned slabs, then rough meadows bright with alpenroses and loud with the cry of marmots. There are streams and boggy patches edged with cotton grass, then vegetation thins out as the trail angles over stony slopes that become steeper on the final twist to the hut. An alternative return is possible on a high path that first visits the Bergsee hut before dropping to the valley.

Lunersee from the Schesaplana

Rätikon Alps

The limestone chain of the Rätikon Alps is gathered in a long wedge of country that is bordered by Liechtenstein, Austria and Switzerland, and it makes for some near-perfect hut-to-hut treks and mountain scrambles at all grades of difficulty. The highest of all its summits is the non-technical 2965 metre Schesaplana, which straddles the Austro-Swiss border, from which the jade-green Lunersee can be seen in marked contrast to the bare grey crests and contorted strata of the mountain. Out of view, but below the Lunersee to the left, runs the Brandnertal, which carries one of the main routes of approach, while the fortress-like peak on the distant right is the Kirchlispitzen. As on the Schesaplana, the south side of that mountain is Swiss and the north flank Austrian. Across both flanks run sections of the very fine Rätikon Höhenweg, a multi-day hut-to-hut tour that could either be made into a circuit that samples both sides of the range or divided into two separate linear routes – one in Switzerland, the other in Austria.

Since the early days of climbing as a form of recreation in the 19th century, many of Europe's most successful mountaineers have served their apprenticeship within the vertical arena of the Eastern Alps. Among their more recent number, these include the Austrians Herman Buhl, Kurt Diemberger and Peter Habeler, as well as Reinhold Messner from the South Tyrol and the Huber brothers, Alexander and Thomas, from München.

Compared with the Mont Blanc range, the Pennines or the Bernese Oberland, the Eastern Alps are minor Alps. They have no summit reaching 4000 metres, and some of their mid-range groups are reminiscent of grass-covered foothills. But a more modest altitude puts no limit on adventure here, for there's no shortage of rock of the most challenging nature, and even outside the Dolomites (which naturally spring to mind) there are extensive playgrounds to explore among the Northern Limestone Alps and the Julians of Slovenia, to name just two districts.

However, there are not only soaring fingers and faces of rock to be found in the Eastern Alps, for a generous variety of landscapes has been spread throughout Austria, Bavaria, northern Italy and Slovenia in numerous groups of such complexity that every type of Alpine scenery known to the South-West and Central Alps is represented here. Plus others.

I think of one particular valley – broad, gently tilted and bearing a dozen shades of green – that leads the eye to a severe wall of blue limestone rising out of forest and appearing from a distance to have a perfectly level crest. The limestone is not blue, of course, but it gives every impression of being so until you draw closer to it. Then you recognize shades of grey, sandy white, ochre and rust-brown, patched here and there with lichen and cushions of pink saxifrage. The crest of this mountain wall is not level either, but broken into turrets and towers, some standing forward of the ridge, others simply exploding from it. Gullies foil any attempt by nature to create uniformity along that wall, and daily one can hear rocks clattering down them to spill onto an apron of scree that fans out from the foot of the cliffs towards invading fingers of alpenrose and dwarf pine.

None of these things is evident from the village on the south side of the valley, nor from the rolling hills that fold upward and on behind the delicately slender spire of its church. I say hills, for that is what they are. Or at least that is the form they take, even though they reach heights greater than anything in Britain; they have neither obvious summit crown nor narrow crest, only broad ridges starred with flowers, and hollows snug with farms.

You can walk up there dressed for summer, along that high grassland, while storm clouds battle the limestone across the way. You can watch the lightning and hear the thunder and feel confident of remaining safe, then turn to the south-east and view distant snowpeaks of the Hohe Tauern across hinted valleys and imagine that you're looking at the Central Alps. With one twist of the neck the Alps' diverse nature is encapsulated in that one sweeping panorama.

The Northern Limestone Alps

Running across the top of Austria and carrying the border with Bavaria, the Kalkalpen, or Northern Limestone Alps, are broken into a series of individual groups as you journey eastward along them. River valleys separate these massifs. Heavy-eaved farms line the banks of the rivers, their meadows massed with rank upon rank of hay-draped trolls in summer, while steep walls of rock burst from their boundaries.

There are deer in the forests and chamois among the upper reaches. Chalets on the summer alps double as restaurants, while scores of mountain huts provide accommodation for walker and climber. The Eastern Alps, better than anywhere in Europe's great arc of mountains, cater for the activist with huts of every size and facility – in Austria alone there are more than 1000.

At either end of the Kalkalpen chain the mountains are green and wooded, but in between the majority of groups exemplify the very best features of limestone country, attractive alike to climber, scrambler, walker and artist. Memories of days spent among the Kaisergebirge, the bewildering karst of the Steinernes Meer, dazzling white rock of the Tennengebirge, and outliers of the Dachstein (to name but a handful) are sufficient to make one's fingers itch for more.

In the centre of Innsbruck you're aware of the presence of mountains. Look above the crowded roofs and you'll see what appears to be an immense wall of rock soaring up and up to the ridge-line of the Karwendelgebirge, a mountain block that carries just one section of the Bavarian border.

Further east the Berchtesgadener Alps range round three sides of the Königsee, giving the lake the appearance of a Norwegian fjord, but the south side of these mountains spills across large areas of limestone pavement that in turn tilts down to alp farms and wooded valleys.

South-east of Salzburg lakes are as much a feature of the landscape as are the mountains, and holidays can be divided between easy lakeside strolls and more energetic journeys up to the high places. Almost everywhere a scene of great beauty cries out for attention.

The Ötztal Alps
Crystalline groups line the borders of Austria and Italy. By contrast with the Northern Limestone Alps, these are snow-crowned and glacier-draped, but like their northern counterparts they are broken into separate districts by river valleys. The Ötztal Alps are a prime example. The Oberinntal flows down the western edge and the Ötztal along the east, while Val Venosta (Vinschgau) effectively contains the district along its southern, Italian, fringe. Inner valleys, such as the Pitztal and Kaunertal, flow north to the River Inn from headwalls of dark rock and gleaming ice, and provide access to some of the best the group has to offer.

For high mountain scenery the Ötztal range is magnificent, and though its summits may not be quite as high as the highest of the Hohe Tauern, the group is abundantly generous, with glacier and snowfield above a foreground of flower meadows. There are several fine huts, tremendous viewpoints and a concentration of glacial peaks, among which the 3772 metre Wildspitze is second only to the Grossglockner as Austria's principal summit.

Crossing the range can be achieved (just) without stepping on a glacier, but there are some high passes and steep trails to contend with; there are huts for overnight accommodation, and landscapes to gladden the eye from start to finish.

The Stubai Alps
East of the Ötztal the Stubai group is named for the valley which drains out of a horseshoe of glacier mountains traced by a pair of renowned

hut-to-hut tours. One tour skirts below the glaciers; the other includes a few summits in its journey. Easily reached within an hour from Innsbruck, the Stubai Alps have known the heavy hand of the ski industry, but by far the larger part of the district has managed to avoid piste scars and mechanical clutter, and remains almost pristine in its blend of snowpeak, tarn, icefield and meadow.

The lower valleys that feed into the main Stubaital are typical of the Tyrol in general, with neat hay meadows, pastures loud with cowbells, and attractive villages almost swamped with flowers at every window. From them paths angle up and across the hillsides; more energetically, some climb over minor cols or trace a route along ridge crests and even visit a few snow-free summits.

While the group is, to all intents and purposes, part of the crystalline range, a kidney-shaped outcrop of limestone erupts from a ridge above Neustift. Viewed across the scree fan that tilts from its base, the Kalkkogel could easily have been transported here from the Dolomites.

Zillertal Alps

The eastern Stubai ends at the Brenner pass, and across that major international road pass rise the first peaks of the Zillertal range. Here again the main crest which carries the frontier is daubed with snow and ice. The highest mountains are of gneiss surrounded by bands of schistose rock. A few of the upper valleys have had their waters dammed for hydro-electric purposes; some of their slopes are dedicated almost entirely to winter sports. But there remains much fine scenery, charming unspoilt valleys to wander through, passes to cross from one country to another, ridges to scramble on, and enough huts to provide excellent multi-day tours far from roads and resorts.

Mayrhofen and Zell-am-Ziller are its major resorts, both of which cater to the ski trade. But come summer and they burst with walkers. And yet, as we have found elewhere, it is not difficult to find peace and space and a sense of solitude among some of the finest mountain scenery – if you're prepared to look for it.

The Tauern Groups

South of the Gerlos pass the Dreiherrenspitze stands astride the Austro-Italian border where the frontier makes a southerly kink to outline the western edge of the Hohe Tauern. Known among mountaineers for the snowy Grossvenediger and Grossglockner peaks, and to naturalists and general tourists for its national park, the Hohe Tauern carries extensive snowfields and glaciers, a tumultuous waterfall and some long ridge systems of firm, trusty rock.

Created in 1984 the Hohe Tauern National Park straddles the provincial borders of Salzburger Land, Carinthia and East Tyrol, and is said to be the largest such park in the Alps. It has more than a 100 summits in excess of 3000 metres high, numerous glaciers, ice caves, about 100 mountain lakes and enough marked trails to satisfy the most energetic of walkers.

The region's outer edge has a number of semi-secluded valleys, as well as a lacework of major highways. Old-time spas have grown into important summer and winter resorts to continue a long tradition of tourism that spills over from the Hohe to the Niedere Tauern. Yet there are peaceful tarn-glinting glens, too, in the heart of the district, and tiny villages unfussed by tourist hype where one can wander or climb in relative seclusion among landscapes of considerable beauty.

The Carnic Alps and Karawanken

While the Lienzer Dolomites stand out north of the broad Gailtal, the Carnic Alps continue the Austro-Italian border towards the frontier shared with Slovenia. The crystalline chain has given way once more to limestone, and a few individual peaks invite comparison with the better-known Dolomites of South Tyrol. Mostly, though, the peaks are unpretentious in scale, forming crusty appendages to green crests above rumpled hills. As with any region there are as many unfrequented parts as there are popular ones, but there are no major resorts to change the character of their warm, welcoming valleys.

East of the Gallitztal the Carnic Alps feed into the Karawanken, a charming group that falls steeply to the Drau on the northern side and into Slovenia on the south. The highest is a modest 2238 metres, and many of the principal peaks have fairly straightforward routes to their summits; but the play of light on their ridges and faces inbues them with a particular kind of beauty that knows neither regret of height nor degree of difficulty.

The Brenta Dolomites

South-east of the Bernina Alps, the Adamello-Presanella group is part of what in the Victorian age Ball and Coolidge referred to as the Lombard Alps. The district is impressive, but its glaciers are retreating at an alarming rate. In their absence lie numerous tarns and pools, and moraines among which nature is busy creating gardens.

Across Valle Rendena, a short morning's walk from the Adamello-Presanella, the landscape is totally different. Here stands a group of exotic multi-coloured crags, towers and spires whose tone and texture appear to change from hour to hour. Though not as extensive or well known as the Dolomites east of the Adige, the Brenta Dolomites are both unique and immensely attractive – a saw-tooth ridge cut in two by the Bocca di Brenta.

Famed for their via ferrata routes, the Brenta have plenty to reward all who are drawn to them – be they climber, scrambler, walker, or those who simply content themselves with a warm rock to sit upon, the bright sun overhead, and as theatrical a scene as nature ever created to gaze upon.

The Dolomites

East of the Adige the main Dolomite range is the most colourful and eccentric in Europe. Douglas Milner referred to their 'ruined masonry', and pointed out that because no streams run through their upper glens, they can be 'ghostly and terrible in their arid silence' (*The Dolomites*). Janet Adam Smith noted 'shocks and freaks of crude pink stone, whose shape, proportion, and colour bear no relation to the valleys from which they spring' (*Mountain Holidays*). Leslie Stephen lay in a meadow at their feet and watched 'the strange transformation of the cliffs [that] would not remain steady for five minutes together' (*The Playground of Europe*).

The Dolomites have indeed become one of the major playgrounds of Europe for climbers, walkers, trekkers, skiers and tourists of every persuasion. They've also been a battleground, and the scars and grim litter of warfare remaining 80 years on.

Roads penetrate where few mountain roads would normally go, and in places the careless motorist can virtually scrape his wing mirror against cliffs that soar above the highway. Elsewhere cableways swing their crowded metal boxes to the summits and shoulders of mountains whose crags would otherwise defy all but the most athletic of climbers and the nesting golden eagle.

All the main Dolomite groups have become honeypots – their huts bursting at the seams in the height of summer, their most popular trails streaming with walkers, and the fashionable climbing routes and via ferratae becoming focal points of attention. But as is the case in every corner of the Alpine chain, there still remain relatively unvisited peaks and valleys to explore, and one may still find a viewpoint of breathtaking splendour on which to sit on a summer's day and imagine the world is yours alone.

The Julian Alps

The 1000 kilometre arc of mountains that began behind Monaco peters out in the wooded hills near Vienna. But the Alps have other endings too, and in the Julians of Slovenia they make perhaps their finest full stop.

In common with the Dolomites these are also limestone mountains, but it's a different limestone, with different colours, shapes and textures. Not less lovely, just different; and their modest altitude belies their impact when seen from one of the outlying valleys. Drained by exquisite clear rivers, with lakes lying in some of them, these Slovene valleys are low, so the peaks seem much higher than they really are. Although nowhere do they reach 3000 metres, the distance from valley bed to summit is similar to that seen among much higher mountains.

The highest is Triglav, whose north face rises 1500 metres out of the Vrata valley, a glen full of wild beauty with mixed woods, lush open meadows and gushing waterfalls. Triglav is a mountain of pilgrimage for the Slovene people, but the same could be said of the Julian Alps everywhere, for these immensely attractive, apparently indestructible mountains seem to represent the spirit of the whole nation.

✳ ✳ ✳

One Sunrise after Another

Day breaks early in June when nights are at their shortest, making it the perfect time for a planned bivouac. Aware of this, three of us left the valley after our evening meal and headed up the dark side of the mountain led by memory, instinct and the distant stars. By the time we reached the summit, the night had only four hours left to run, so we huddled among a nest of rocks to watch the stars spin their course.

At last those far-off pinpricks of light were extinguished one by one, the eastern sky mellowed, and the sun sprang from its resting place to flood the world with its glory, bleeding on summit snows and staining hillsides with extravagant promise.

Inspired by the scene we scurried down slopes of snow to gain a second sunrise, then another. There were rocky patches, then grass as the gradient eased, with the sun now casting its warmth and benediction over all the Eastern Alps as far as the eye could see – range upon range of wave-like peaks rising out of shadow into the light of a new day.

We came to the first farm, isolated on a grassy lip with forest below, with the mountain above and the sun full ahead. The farmer's wife stood at the open door drawing strength from the sunshine, her face reflecting its warmth. 'Where have you been?' she asked. I told her. 'It was good?'

'Wunderschön!'

Invited to breakfast, we carried a small table out of the house and covered it with a cloth, plates and bowls. Her husband finished milking the cows and joined us. We ate home-made bread spread with home-made butter and jam, and drank bowls of coffee, thick with fresh milk.

'Isn't this a bit early to be up and working?' I asked in innocence.

'We have no clock,' remarked the woman. 'When the sun shines through our window to warm the bed, we get up.'

Taschachferner from the Fuldaer Höhenweg

Ötztal Alps

Extensive snowfields and glaciers add stature to the Ötztal Alps, with scenes to parallel those of many districts in the Central and South-West Alps. These are mountains that would repay a visit from would-be alpinists, for they have all the features – and some of the hazards – one would expect to find on larger peaks, but without the degree of commitment required, say, to climb in the Mont Blanc range or parts of the Bernese or Pennine Alps. They should not be under-estimated, however, for they are still serious mountains. Visually, of course, they are no second-best, and the walker is spoilt for choice as far as single-day outings and hut-to-hut tours are concerned. This photograph of the Taschachferner spilling down from the Wildspitze massif was taken from the Fuldaer Höhenweg during a three-day crossing of the range, the previous night having been spent in the German Alpine Club's Taschachhaus, which is used as a base for climbing courses and by climbers tackling ice routes on the neighbouring peaks.

Ice pool below the Wildspitze

Ötztal Alps

Between the Taschachhaus and Ölgrubenjoch the upper reaches of the Taschachtal are hemmed in by steep slopes and glaciers. Caught among the folds of an old moraine lies a small tarn that remains semi-frozen well into the summer. From its bank there is an unobstructed view up the snow-covered glacier to the Wildspitze, Austria's second-highest peak at 3772 metres. We had approached it from above, having crossed the 3095 metre Ölgrubenjoch from the Gepatsch Haus in the Kaunertal, and this was virtually the last of the ice on our route. From a distance the moraine bank that walled the tarn appeared to be nothing but a barren sprawl of rocky debris, but on close inspection it revealed a surprising variety of plants that had translated the wilderness into a true rock garden. Then, as we descended beyond that and came to a green baize of meadow, there were more flowers and butterflies, and young marmots romping under the watch of fat adults. In a few short hours we had walked out of winter, through spring and into summer.

The Kalkkogel massif

Stubai Alps

Conveniently reached by public transport from Innsbruck, the Stubai Alps extend the chain east of the Ötztal range as far as the Brenner pass. Like their neighbours to the west, as far as the Eastern Alps are concerned these are 'big' 3000 metre mountains, many of which are heavily clothed with snow and ice. And like the Ötztal, the Stubai is mostly a crystalline range, yet on its northern edge the Kalkkogel is an outburst of limestone reminiscent of the Dolomites. When tackling the classic Stubai Circuit – a hut-to-hut tour par excellence – the penultimate stage crosses the extensive scree fan seen here on the way to the Starkenberger hut above Neustift. An exciting aerial view of these mountains is to be had when approaching Innsbruck by air, for they form part of the corridor through which aircraft make their final run. From the ground, of course, they are no less exciting, the soft weathered rock erupting as a forest of towers and gesticulating fingers from sun-bleached screes.

Grunausee and the Wilder Freiger

Stubai Alps

Right across the Alpine chain retreating glaciers are leaving in their wake a dazzling collection of tarns such as the Grunausee, with its glorious view of the Wilder Freiger. This scene is a feature of the Stubai Circuit, during a day that crosses a rocky ridge and descends a series of shallow ledges below the Niederl, on the stage that journeys between the Nürnberger hut and the Sulzenau. Making an extensive horseshoe tour of the Stubai Alps over a week or more – depending which huts are used – the route keeps well away from roads and villages in order to explore the very best of the district. Overnight accommodation is to be had in a diverse assortment of mountain huts, all of which provide meals and refreshments, so one can travel light, unencumbered by camping equipment or food. A similar tour virtually parallels this walker's route but, keeping higher, it travels across the glaciers and collects several summits on the way.

The Kuchelmooskar basin below the Plauener hut

Zillertal Alps

The Zillergrund is one of the more remote and romantic valleys of the Zillertal Alps. Above the Bärenbad inn a private road served by bus from Mayrhofen snakes up to a reservoir dam which acts as the starting point for an approach to the Plauener hut. Overlooking the cliff-rimmed Kuchelmooskar cirque, the hut was originally built at the end of the 19th century; it has since been enlarged and can now accommodate 80 in its dormitories. It rests on a steep slope on the edge of the cirque with an exemplary view of a great maze of crags, ridges, summits and hinted valleys. Halfway to it from the dam, and immediately before the trail begins its long zigzag climb, the way crosses the Keesbach torrent within the Kuchelmooskar basin. In early summer alpenroses blaze among hillocks of dwarf pine, and the crags are starred with tiny clusters of alpine flowers. Passing beneath the bridge, the glacial torrent surges over a lip and pours down the hillside before spilling into the milky reservoir several hundred metres below.

Stilluptal from above Mayrhofen

Zillertal Alps

It is claimed that the Zillertal and its tributaries have around 1700 kilometres of marked walking routes, which helps to explain the popularity in summer of resorts like Zell am Ziller and Mayrhofen. The range of these walks – and the scenic quality of its valleys – is indeed impressive. There are gentle valley strolls among flower meadows or alongside streams, mid-height roller-coaster trails, ridge-walks, pass crossings and a multi-day hut-to-hut tour to equal that of the neighbouring Stubai Alps. Huts used on this tour can also be visited on day walks by taking a bus to a valley mouth then spending a few hours aiming towards the ice peaks that rim the valley head, at the foot of which most of the huts can be found. Directly above Mayrhofen, where this photograph was taken, there are no huts, but having cable access it attracts plenty of walkers. From the lip of the ridge three friends contemplate the Stilluptal opposite, which also has a number of routes worth tackling.

Sunset colours from the Hundstein

Dientner Berge

Folding between the Steinernes Meer and the Salzach river valley east of Zell am See, a series of mostly rounded, often grass-covered mountains form a gentle buffer zone between the severe Northern Limestone Alps and the snowy Tauern range. Like the neighbouring Kitzbüheler Alps that spread west of the Saalach valley, there's practically no climbing to be had here, but the walking potential is immense and with special appeal to those who might otherwise feel intimidated by the Alpine scale of higher districts. This image was captured from the Statzerhaus, a simple manned hut built on the 2117 metre summit of the Hundstein above Thumersbach. On the way to it I had been overtaken by a summer storm when on a particularly exposed ridge section. Thankful that I was not among bigger mountains, I found new energy and scurried to the hut with a surge of adrenalin. The storm died at sunset as a soft golden light sank across the hills and drained into the valleys in an act of penance.

Sun-bleached peaks above Werfenweng

Tennengebirge

South-east of Salzburg, and not an hour's journey from the city, the Tennengebirge is a small, compact group of mountains within the long Kalkalpen chain, known as the Northern Limestone Alps. The limestone here is bleached and virtually snow-free in summer, and in common with most of this range the mountains burst from rucked pastureland with a boldness to match that of the Dolomites of South Tyrol. On three sides woods and pastures ripple across the lower slopes and encourage footpaths. Above Werfenweng meadows grazed by both cattle and horses are measured by trails that creep along the base of the crags, while others suggest steeper, more challenging ways into the heartland, where a number of manned huts provide accommodation in a wild and seemingly remote setting. While on the surface the karst adopts different colours and complexions painted hour by hour by the sun, within the mountains themselves there's a complex system of caves, including the world's largest ice cave measuring some 40-odd kilometres.

Val Brenta Alta

Brenta Dolomites

Separated from the main Dolomite groups by the Adige river valley, the Brenta district astounds with abrupt crags, turrets and fortresses. Freshfield wrote of 'Towers of Babel'. Walker spoke of 'flaming walls of masonry … a mountain world … of surpassing grandeur', while countless others have sung its praise in extravagant prose. For a long time one of the least known Alpine districts, its reputation for theatricality and sheer drama is now assured, so solitude is no longer one of the Brenta's gifts. The fame of its scenery, and the spectacular nature of its walks, climbs and via ferrata routes, ensures that it is extremely busy with visitors. Approached from Madonna di Campiglio, Val Brenta entices with its fairytale backdrop. Seen here from the vicinity of Rifugio Alberto ai Brentei, bizarre sentry-like towers and buttresses guard the inner glen leading to the pass of Bocca di Brenta. Disappearing out of the frame to the right, the dark shape rises to Cima Tosa, highest of the Brenta group, climbed in 1865 by John Ball, first president of the Alpine Club.

Sella Group above Passo Gardena

The Dolomites

The massive Sella Group consists of an apparently solid central mountain block topped by a high plateau and surrounded by rank upon rank of flat-topped, vertical-walled campaniles famed as the Sella Towers. As the area is ringed by roads that scrape alongside some of these towers, a few of which are strung with cableways and overlooked by four major passes – Sella, Gardena, Campolungo and Pordoi, one would be forgiven for thinking that there are no secrets left. But seen from an assortment of trails that weave among outlying districts, the Sella comes into its own, displaying as it does the complex nature of its construction. It then becomes obvious that it would take many long weeks of dedicated but rewarding exploration to fully unravel the maze of hidden corners that include valleys slicing deep into the fortress-like massif. There are paths aplenty and airy via ferrata routes too, and a barren desert of stone to explore across the vast summit plateau. In fact the Sella Group would keep an inquisitive walker happy for a full summer's roaming.

Dolomitic rock fingers near Passo Cir

The Dolomites

A moonscape of dolomitic rock confuses a trail that weaves its way between gesticulating fingers and spires below Passo Cir. Across a hidden valley the Sella Group forms a powerful backdrop and brings to the landscape a sense of permanence that is absent among these crumbling foreground formations. Echoes rattle among the hollows, and dust rises from slopes of scree whenever a breeze intrudes. But although one's first impression may be of a mountain boneyard, a charnel house where nothing lives, it takes but a few moments of reflection to notice exquisite flowering plants nodding from tiny cleavages of rock, or the cushions of saxifrage that spread across the screes. Insects are at home in this strangest of uplands, and with a rush of feathers birds, too, announce their presence among the ancient, crumbling bones of mountains between whose ancestors fish once swam. The trail at bottom left is a popular one that begins above Passo Gardena and, crossing a diverse landscape, leads to Rifugio Puez as part of the long-distance Alta Via 2.

Mont de Seura

The Dolomites

The crest of Mont de Seura rises from a long scree apron over which well-trodden paths add their scars. Val Chedul spills away from the screes down to the right, draining eventually to Selva in Val Gardena, while Passo Cir is hidden by the prominent thumb-like projection on the ridge crest. An initial steep descent from the pass brings a trail tight against the crags before easing across the screes to the vantage point, from which this photograph was taken, a little below the next ridge, which is crossed at the 2528 metre Passo Crespëina. In the far distance, and partially concealed by Mont de Seura, the big block of the Sassolunga – or Langkofel – can be seen. Standing at the very head of Val Gardena, the Sassolunga is one of its most prominent features, and around it a series of trails can be linked to make a wonderful full-day's tour; in fact the Gardena district is one of the finest in all the Dolomites from a walker's point of view, with views to match.

Rifugio Locatelli

The Dolomites

Seen from the bare, windblown saddle of the Forcella di Lavaredo at 2457 metres, Rifugio Antonio Locatelli is dwarfed by the Torre di Toblin. Facing south the Locatelli – or Drei-Zinnen-Hütte – is a sizeable inn-like refuge famed for its full-frontal view of the Tre Cima. Of the many fine trails in the neighbourhood, that old Dolomite connoisseur Douglas Milner favoured one that descends west to Valle di Landro; while the most oft-used route of approach must surely be the one that cuts across the foreground scree slope through shadows cast by Monte Paterno – also known as the Paternkofel. Many Dolomite features have two names, of course, as a result of border changes that occurred after the end of the First World War, when the South Tyrol was transferred from Austria to Italy. And of all Alpine districts, it is the Dolomites that carries the history of that war as a vast outdoor museum; trenches, tunnels and even a number of via ferrata routes owe their origins to that conflict.

Tre Cima di Lavaredo

The Dolomites

Perhaps the most famous, and certainly the most easily recognized, of the Dolomite peaks, the Tre Cima di Lavaredo reveal different aspects of their character as you work your way round them. Seen from the Forcella di Lavaredo at the left-hand end of the picture, the Cima Piccolissima seems to erupt from a pedestal of scree. When viewed from the north the individual peaks are given due prominence and respect, while in the image here, taken on the approach to Forcella Col di Mezzo, the mountains display a solid, well-planed aspect. In the foreground is Sasso di Landro. Then comes Cima Ovest – its highly respected north face in shadow; its west face lit by the afternoon sunshine. Though 25 metres higher than its neighbour, Cima Grande appears inferior to Cima Ovest, while Punta di Frida and Cima Piccolissima are dwarfed in the distance. Not surprisingly, the Tre Cima contain some of the most exacting Dolomite climbs, but the trails that skirt below them also reward with visually exciting walks – so there's something here for everyone.

Monte Cristallo

The Dolomites

Rising directly above the Tre Croci road pass near Cortina d'Ampezzo, Monte Cristallo is the dominant mountain of this busiest of Dolomite resorts. First climbed in 1865 by the Austrian Paul Grohmann with two Cortina guides, a number of the early pioneers were struck by the impressive beauty of this 3221 metre peak. F.F. Tuckett, for example, who was one of the foremost explorers of the Alps and who made its second ascent, called it 'a most glorious peak … the Cristallo struck me as finer than the Géant from Courmayeur'. G.C. Churchill, who with Josiah Gilbert wrote the classic book *The Dolomite Mountains* in 1864, described the Cristallo from the north as 'shooting up in towers between its glaciers'. Seen here from the Sorapiss massif to the south, the mountain is being battered by wild autumnal winds. As cloud shadows raced across its flanks, it appeared to be moving with them. To the right of the deep gash of the Passo del Cristallo rises the spire of Piz Popena at 3152 metres, marking the massif's south-east cornerstone.

The Carnic, Karawanken and Julian Alps

Carnic Alps

In the scorching brilliance of an early summer's morning, among the confused topography of the Eastern Alps, where the boundaries of Austria, Italy and Slovenia are drawn along ridge crests, a gap in a wooded saddle provides a lookout towards the merging of Carnic, Karawanken and Julian Alps. This is limestone country that continues where the Dolomites give way, and it is cleft with deep ravines whose rivers shine with water-polished, humbug-striped boulders. Forests hug the lower slopes, interspersed with meadows full of flowers in springtime; from the end of June to early August it's possible to find the rare *Wulfenia Carinthiaca* – a deep blue bell-flower that is highly protected. Above the meadows and lonely alp farms, above scree tips and boulder-fields, jaunty little peaks protrude, around which the Carnic (or Karnischer) Höhenweg weaves a multi-day tour along the ridges and high pastures of this straggling chain. On the north slope of the Nassfeld pass, Sonnenalpe Nassfeld is well known in Carinthia for winter skiing and summer walking, while activists from both Austria and Italy mingle on neighbourhood summits.

The Seven Lakes valley

Julian Alps

Defining one of the eastern boundaries of the Alpine chain – another stretches almost to Vienna – the Julian Alps straddle the borders of Italy and Slovenia. Slovenia claims the lion's share, with a knot of mountains whose intertwining valleys sparkle with lakes and some of the purest streams to be found anywhere in Europe. Broadleaved forests clothe many of these valleys, opening to flower meadows with scattered barns and small villages. Triglav, the highest of its peaks at 2864 metres, is something of a national symbol. To reach its summit is almost an act of pilgrimage for Slovenes, and a national park has been created around it to protect both the mountain and much of its neighbourhood. The delectable Seven Lakes valley – Dolina Triglavskih Jezer – rimmed by stark limestone walls, is included within the park and is visited on one of the many routes to Triglav's summit. Between two of the lakes there is a popular three-storey hut with places for 200 and a junction of trails is close by.

Prisojnik

Julian Alps

Typical of the Julian heartland, impressive shadow-washed peaks crowd the head of the Velika Pisnika valley south of Kranjska Gora. The mountains are not high by Alpine standards – Prisojnik is only 2547 metres – but the valleys are low so that the peaks seem much higher than they really are, and they have an indefinable majesty that is unrelated to mere statistics of elevation. According to the late Dudley Stevens, who in the 1960s led many expeditions there, the Julians are formed 'mostly of karst limestone, a beautiful but unstable white rock which is enticing for photographers and exhilarating for mountain walkers, but suspect in places for climbing' (*The Mountains of Europe*). The Slovenes are passionate about their mountains and have created a network of long-distance routes which lead from summit to summit, from valley to valley and from hut to hut to enable the active visitor to absorb some of the magic of this truly enchanting region. Without question it counts as one of the most delightful of the whole Alpine chain, and has an atmosphere all its own.

On a July day in 1861 Auguste Bisson, along with Auguste Balmat as his guide and a caravan of no less than 25 porters labouring under a mass of equipment weighing several hundredweight, set out for the summit of Mont Blanc intent on obtaining the first-ever photographs of the view from the crown of the Alps. To achieve just three successful images, Bisson would have used a cumbersome tripod camera, black cloth hood, glass plates measuring 20 inches by 16, a tent to act as a portable darkroom, plus a quantity of chemicals and fresh water with which to process his negatives right there on the mountain. Compare that to the modern photographer with his compact digital camera whose images can be stored, edited or discarded in an instant.

But in the century and a half between these extremes certain elements remain constant. The first is the visual appeal of a mountain landscape, while the second is the need for sufficient light to capture the chosen image. In addition to these two basic ingredients, a third is then required in order to create a photograph that will inspire, excite or instruct – the photographer's 'eye for a picture'.

An Eye for a Picture

In almost a century and a half since Bisson's pioneering achievement, a number of talented practitioners with that essential eye for a picture have produced many memorable images from the outdoor studio of the Alps. W.F. Donkin, who in 1879 listed Alpine photography as one of his qualifications for membership of the Alpine Club, was among the first. By the time he lost his life in the Caucasus in 1888, he had managed to turn mountain photography into an art form, and one can only speculate on what he might have achieved had he had the benefit of more portable equipment. His Italian contemporary Vittorio Sella was another early master who created matchless portraits in black and white that retain the power to excite, even today, when in our present age the sheer scale of the mountain world can be projected onto an IMAX screen with images large enough to include the viewer in the action.

With so many of his finest photographs being reproduced in books of Alpine exploration by such eminent climber-authors as Coolidge and Freshfield, Sella awakened public interest in the mountain landscape. With his own unique vision, he managed to convey both the magnitude and the beauty of the Alps better than anyone before him. Ronald Clark called Sella 'the master of the set-piece mountain panorama [in which] splendid profiles stand in bold relief.... There are horizons without end, and one can almost hear the voices of the old climbers in the still air' (*Mountaineering*).

Colour or Black and White?

Today almost everyone uses colour – whether they are creating print or transparency film, or reproducing a digital image – but black and white can and does create dramatic effects among the Alps. Look at the moody photographs produced by Frank Smythe, whose pre-war books inspired generations of climbers and armchair adventurers alike, and the work of the American Bradford Washburn, who specializes in aerial photography. The latter's genius has never been more forcefully represented than in his exciting view of a rope of six tiny climbers on the east ridge of the Doldenhorn, silhouetted against a cloud bank. It is without question one of the finest of all mountain images, being perfectly composed and perfectly lit; it is at once a revelation and a challenge to all who go among wild places with a camera. In a single frame, Washburn's eye for a picture has managed to record the transient nature of the clouds, the harsh beauty of the high Alps and the adventure of mountaineering.

With Mont Blanc on his doorstep, Pierre Tairraz comes from a long family line of mountain photographers. It is claimed that his great-grandfather, Joseph, a guide, one-time Mayor of Chamonix and a photographer, actually took seven negatives from the summit of Mont Blanc before August Bisson. When Pierre teamed up with the well-known guide Gaston Rébuffet to make the film 'Between Heaven and Earth' ('Entre Terre et Ciel'), which won the Grand Prix at the Trento International Mountain Film Festival in 1961, and whose stills were subsequently used in a highly successful book, Tairraz established a reputation for his ability to portray not only the full drama and romance of wild landscapes, but also the actions of climbers that were hinted at in Washburn's Doldenhorn masterpiece.

Painting with Light

What makes these photographers stand out from the crowd is sheer dedication to their craft; the ability to interpret light as well as landscape; and a determination to capture the essential mood of their subject, no matter how long it may take. Each had an instinctive personal vision, and by creating an individual style also managed to stamp his own unmistakable signature on his work.

Others who have similarly turned mountain photography into a true art form, and whose work is instantly recognized as bearing the mark of individuality, include the Swiss Willi Burkhardt, whose work with a large-format camera has produced a wonderful collection of mountain portraits (examples can be seen in *The High Mountains of the Alps*). Then there's John Cleare, whose work spans several decades of inspirational photography, both of climbers in action and crisp images of mountains around the world. Wilderness photographer John Beatty has a uniquely poetic touch, beautifully expressed in his audio-visual presentations. And there's the late Galen Rowell, whose 1986 book *Mountain Light* (subtitled: *In search of the dynamic landscape*) is the ultimate textbook that all aspiring mountain photographers should drool over. In it, he not only explains techniques and mechanical detail, but describes how he achieved certain extraordinary images and the emotions that inspired them.

Using what Comes Naturally

A good photographer needs no sophisticated equipment to create memorable images, as I discovered some years ago when I made a series of mountain journeys with Peter Smith, a good friend who happens to be one of the country's foremost architectural photographers. On one of these journeys he carried an uncomplicated Olympus Trip compact camera that fitted neatly in his pocket, together with a supply of monochrome film. It was an enlightening experience, photography-wise, and a morning spent in his darkroom afterwards produced stunning poster-sized mountain portraits that would stand out in any exhibition.

From watching Pete at work, and from acting on occasion as his model, I learnt several lessons, perhaps the most important of which was to predict a scene, situation or condition of light that would make a rewarding composition. As an example of this he would see a cloud shadow drifting slowly across the landscape, predict where it would be at a given moment, and either position his camera to exploit that shadow or the cloud it represented, or place a figure in the landscape in such a way as to draw attention to it. In these and other carefully considered ways his mountains and valleys came alive; they became part of a moving world, not static monuments of nature.

I make no claims for my own efforts with a camera, except to confess that I gain tremendous enjoyment from the actual process of taking photographs, especially in a wild landscape. Being among mountains in all weathers is a privilege and a never-fading pleasure; but aside from living each moment there, I want to interpret what I experience in the very face of nature when seen in all its unadorned beauty, and to use my camera both as a canvas and an addition to memory. My aim is to create a picture or an emotion that stores a specific moment in time – one that can later be cast upon a screen or printed in a book, and through which I can relive that moment, recalling both for myself and my audience the sounds, the scents and sensations at work when that image was first gathered.

Photography is also an important adjunct to my work as a writer of guidebooks, the words and images being used to complement each other in an attempt to describe or interpret a landscape.

That being said, I firmly believe that unless you're taking photographs for a living, it's essential to keep the whole photographic process in perspective; allow your camera to add something to the mountain experience, not dominate or impede it. For experience is a gift to be treasured and, as was suggested elsewhere in this book, we should try to become aware of every aspect of the world about us – to absorb the environment, not simply scan it and pass on. This can only happen if we use all our senses, rather than concentrate on the visual to the exclusion of all else.

By focusing the world through a camera lens, and being tied to the f-stop mechanics of taking pictures, it's possible to lose touch with reality.

The Moment of Truth

At the close of lectures to camera clubs I always dread the first question from my audience, for invariably members of that audience will know far more about the techniques of photography than I. This, then, is the moment of truth, so my reaction to technical questions has to be straightforward and honest. To me photography is instinctive, but it relies for effectiveness on the following simple rules.

- Know your camera – its strengths and weaknesses (this only comes from regular use in all conditions).
- Know the film you're using – its limitations and what you can get away with, given available light.
- Make sure you have a film in your camera.
- Develop an eye for a picture (study the work of master photographers to see what works).
- Most importantly – be in the right place at the right time.

Note i: The vast majority of photographs reproduced in this book were taken on Kodachrome 25 – a film noted for fine-grained images, and a perfect medium for projecting onto large theatre-sized screens. Sadly, in 2001 Kodak ceased production of this film.

Note ii: In addition to Galen Rowell's *Mountain Light* mentioned above, an excellent handbook for the outdoor enthusiast wishing to take better landscape, wildlife or action photographs is *Outdoor Photography* by Jon Sparks (Cicerone, 2002).

RECOMMENDED READING

Alpine bibliographies can fill complete volumes, for just about every district and every aspect of the mountains has been described in print several times over. The following list must therefore be selective, but it includes titles that have proved to be either entertaining or instructive.

Adam Smith, Janet *Mountain Holidays* (Dent, 1946/The Ernest Press, 1997) A charming account of pre-war climbing holidays in Scotland and the Alps. Evocative of an era long gone, but with some districts surprisingly unchanged.

Clark, Ronald W. *The Alps* (Weidenfeld & Nicolson, 1973) An entertaining collection of essays by a well-known mountain historian.

Clark, Ronald W. *The Splendid Hills* (Phoenix House, 1948) The life and photographs of Vittorio Sella.

Dumler, Helmut & Burkhardt, Willi *The High Mountains of the Alps* (Diadem, 1993) A beautifully produced volume which illustrates the Alpine 4000m peaks.

Freshfield, D.W. *Italian Alps* (Longmans, 1875/Blackwell, 1937) Travels by a Victorian pioneer in the Lepontine and Bregaglia Alps, among others.

Irving, R.L.G. *The Alps* (Batsford, 1939) Long out of print, but available on special loan from some libraries or via internet book-search sites, this volume by a noted Alpine connoisseur covers the whole range.

Kugy, Julius *Alpine Pilgrimage* (Murray, 1934) A fascinating book by an Austrian climber whose love of the Julian Alps was particularly revealing.

Lieberman, Marcia R. *The Outdoor Traveler's Guide: The Alps* (Stewart, Tabori & Chang, New York 1991) With numerous fine illustrations by Tim Thompson, much of the Alpine chain is described.

Maeder, Herbert *The Mountains of Switzerland* (George Allen & Unwin, 1968) A large-format book of monochrome photographs that illustrate the Swiss Alps from a climber's perspective.

Moore, A.W. *The Alps in 1864* (latest edition in 2 vols, Blackwell, 1939) Moore was with Whymper and Horace Walker during the summer of 1864.

Moran, Martin *Alps 4000* (David & Charles, 1994) An account of Moran's and Simon Jenkins' epic journey across all the 4000m summits of the Alps.

Poucher, W.A. *The Alps* (Constable, 1983) Contains 100 colour photographs of major Alpine peaks and general mountain scenes.

Reynolds, Kev *Walking in the Alps* (Cicerone Press, 1998) An attempt to bring Walker (see below) up to date. The whole range is described in 19 chapters.

Walker, J. Hubert *Walking in the Alps* (Oliver & Boyd, 1951) A splendid book of inspiration. Walker describes selected regions in beautiful prose.

Whymper, Edward *Scrambles Amongst the Alps* (many editions) This is the classic volume of mountaineering literature covering Whymper's Alpine campaigns from 1860 to 1865.

ABOUT THE AUTHOR

Known to walkers and trekkers as a prolific author of guidebooks to the Alps, Pyrenees and Himalaya, Kev Reynolds is also a photojournalist whose images have appeared in numerous books by other writers, as well as in magazines, advertisements, tourist office brochures, calenders and greetings cards. A member of the Alpine Club, Austrian Alpine Club and Outdoor Writers' Guild, and the first honorary member of the British Association of European Mountain Leaders (BAEML), his passion for mountains remains undiminished after a lifetime's activity. When not climbing or trekking in one of the world's great ranges, Kev lives among what he calls the 'Kentish Alps', and during the winter months regularly travels throughout Britain to share his love for wild places with a variety of audiences through his lectures. Check him out on www.kevreynolds.co.uk

Alpine guidebooks by the author – published by Cicerone Press

Walking in the Alps	100 Hut Walks in the Alps
Walks in the Engadine	Walking in the Valais
The Bernese Alps	Walking in Ticino
Central Switzerland	Écrins National Park
Tour of the Vanoise	Tour of Mont Blanc
Chamonix to Zermatt, the Walker's Haute Route	Alpine Pass Route

LISTING OF CICERONE GUIDES

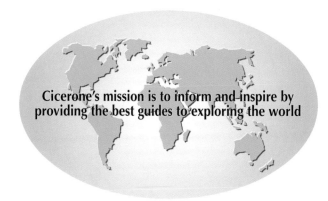

Cicerone's mission is to inform and inspire by providing the best guides to exploring the world

Since its foundation over 30 years ago, Cicerone has specialised in publishing guidebooks and has built a reputation for quality and reliability. It now publishes nearly 300 guides to the major destinations for outdoor enthusiasts, including Europe, UK and the rest of the world.

Written by leading and committed specialists, Cicerone guides are recognised as the most authoritative. They are full of information, maps and illustrations so that the user can plan and complete a successful and safe trip or expedition – be it a long face climb, a walk over Lakeland fells, an alpine traverse, a Himalayan trek or a ramble in the countryside.

With a thorough introduction to assist planning, clear diagrams, maps and colour photographs to illustrate the terrain and route, and accurate and detailed text, Cicerone guides are designed for ease of use and access to the information.

If the facts on the ground change, or there is any aspect of a guide that you think we can improve, we are always delighted to hear from you.

Cicerone Press
2 Police Square Milnthorpe Cumbria LA7 7PY
Tel:01539 562 069   Fax:01539 563 417
e-mail:info@cicerone.co.uk   web:www.cicerone.co.uk

CICERONE